Rev. Jack A. Kent is a Unitarian minister,
communities in various locations on the Ea
in New York, Chicago, Washington and Va   ....ology
at the universities of California and Chicago, and after seeing active service in the
USA Air Force during the Second World War, he gained his M Div from Starr King
School for the Ministry, Berkeley, California, in 1950. In addition to being a Unitarian
minister, he held a number of high-ranking positions in industry, commerce and administration. He has written numerous articles, is a regular contributor to theological
journals, and stands in the vanguard of what is known as the radical reformation.

Jack Kent is married, has a son and two daughters, and now lives on Hornby Island,
British Columbia. His hobbies include carving in wood and stone.

The Psychological Origins of the Resurrection Myth

Jack A. Kent

OPEN GATE PRESS
LONDON

First published in 1999 by Open Gate Press
51 Achilles Road, London NW6 1DZ

British Library Cataloguing-in-Publication Programme
A catalogue record for this book is available from the British Library.

ISBN 1 871871 43 3

Printed in Great Britain by
Redwood Books, Trowbridge, Wiltshire

CONTENTS

PREFACE

In many ways I am indebted to the work of Joseph Campbell, who has advised humanity that the myths from previous generations carry the deepest wisdom of the human race. The formative myths from earlier societies speak to the inner life of the human spirit, and one of the tasks of every human being is to understand the messages our inherited myths carry for us today.

Since I was born into a family which was very active in a fundamentalist Methodist Church, my early spiritual inheritance was one of Christian fundamentalism. I can well remember that as a child my mother would always insist that the entire family must go to the Easter sunrise service, where we would stand in the early morning light waiting for the return of the resurrected Jesus Christ.

In my university years I rebelled against the obvious shallowness of the myths of my childhood, because they were presented to me as dogmatic instructions. Furthermore, the insights which were contained in the myths were ruined because of the interpretation which was so often given by ministers who were working by rote.

Now, in the forty-ninth year of my ministry, I am able to look back with a new and more comfortable view of my own, and look for the psychological insights which might be gleaned by those who are not afraid to look at the old stories from a new and different point of view.

Joseph Campbell, quoting Carl Jung, has warned us that we cannot go back to our inherited myths as we once knew them, because they will draw us away from the world of modern consciousness. What is required is a dialogue between our old myths and symbolic forms, and modern consciousness and knowledge. It is this process, alone, which will provide the opportunity of mining the old myths for their modern relevance.

It is in this spirit that I present the following work.

Jack A. Kent
Hornby Island, B.C.
Canada

19 March 1999

ACKNOWLEDGEMENTS

Many people played a role in the development and writing of this book. My greatest thanks must be extended to Nellis Shakleton and to Diane Brown who shared many of their ideas and life experiences with me. Without them this book would never have been written.

I am also indebted to Dr John Whitworth and Dr Michael Kenny who are members of the Department of Sociology and Anthropology at Simon Fraser University. They gave me a lot of their time when I needed to have some guidance from the academic world.

I am especially indebted to Dr Cath Gray who gave me steadfast support as well as advising me on the logical structure and the major issues and arguments as they are presented in this book.

Dr Robert Kimball, Dean of Starr King School for the Ministry in Berkeley, California from 1968 to 1998, has been a steadfast friend and consultant. His strength and guidance have given me encouragement and direction. Starr King School for the Ministry is a member of the Graduate Theological Union in Berkeley, California.

In a more technical sense there have been some very special people who were willing to talk with me about the details of this work. They are: Dr William Halladay, Dr Stephen R Shuchter, Professor Antony Flew, Dr Stan Garber, Mr Brian Scrivener, Mr Ray Grigg, Mr Jake Banky, Dr Raymond Archer, Dr Will Stone, and Mr John Walls.

I must also thank my wife, Barbara, who has encouraged and helped me in this very long endeavour.

All biblical quotes are from the *Oxford Annotated Bible: Revised Standard Version* unless otherwise indicated.

Chapter 1

Resurrection as the Basis of Christian Faith

The purpose of this book is to give the psychological reasons why Mary Magdalene, the disciples, and the apostle Paul believed that a human being, Jesus of Nazareth, was resurrected from the dead by God.

I approach this work with considerable apprehension because it will be a challenge to the wider Christian community. The mainline Christian churches want to update their theology in the light of modern knowledge, but the acceptance of contemporary psychology when it is applied to the founding events of Christianity is very threatening to its basic theology.[1] The Christian fundamentalists will surely say that the denial of the actual physical resurrection of Jesus of Nazareth is heretical. The liberal religionists need to look at the old doctrines of the Resurrection, the Ascension and the Pentecost, Paul's deep faith in Jesus Christ, and the doctrine of the Holy Trinity from a new and different point of view. I maintain that Christianity and its many branches are an important part of the religious heritage of the Western world and any effort to shed new light on the origins of Christianity should be welcomed by every denomination.

It is my hope that a new psychological interpretation of well-known yet mostly neglected evidence contained in the New Testament will clarify why the physical resurrection of Jesus never occurred and why the myth of the Resurrection, the Ascension and the Pentecost came into existence and continues to be a very important myth in the spiritual life of the West.

However, before I proceed I want to pay tribute to the distinguished German theologian Christian Hermann Weisse who, writing in 1838, first proposed a psychological approach to the resurrection. His works are not available to me, but Albert Schweitzer, in his *Quest of the Historical Jesus*, reviewed Weisse's book *A Critical and*

1

Philosophical Study of the Gospel History. My book was completed before I found the following quotes in Schweitzer's work. Weisse wrote:

> The historical fact [of the resurrection] is only the existence of a belief, not the belief of the later Christian Church in the myth of the bodily resurrection of the Lord but the personal belief of the Apostles and their companions in the miraculous presence of the risen Christ in the visions and appearances which they experienced... The question whether those extraordinary phenomena which, soon after the death of the Lord, actually and undeniably took place within the community of His disciples rest upon fact or illusion, that is, whether in them the departed spirit of the Lord, of whose presence the disciples supposed themselves to be conscious, was really present, or whether the phenomena were produced by natural causes of a different kind, spiritual and psychical, is a question which cannot be answered without going beyond the confines of purely historical criticism. [*It is certain*] *that the resurrection of Jesus is a fact which belongs to the domain of the spiritual and psychic life, and which is not related to outward corporeal existence in such a way that the body which was laid in the grave could have shared therein.* (Schweitzer, pp.130-131, my italics)

Schweitzer then wrote: 'Weisse... was the first to handle the problem from a point of view which combined historical with psychological considerations, and he was fully conscious of the novelty and the far-reaching consequences of his attempt. Theological science did not overtake him for 60 years' (Schweitzer, p.131).

I believe it is important to follow Weisse's approach and use contemporary grief studies and psychiatry to attempt another psychological approach to the founding events in the Christian church. This is necessary because psychological knowledge has advanced far beyond the information which was available to Weisse in 1838. In addition, the Christian myth has been a part of the psychological inheritance of Western civilization and when we understand the origins of the myth we can approach it with a new, yet different, level of appreciation.

The Christian faith is grounded in the belief that Jesus of Nazareth was crucified and buried, and on the third day was resurrected from the dead by a unilateral act of God. Thus, Jesus of Nazareth became the Christ of faith.

The classical summary statement of the Christian faith is found in the apostle Paul's first letter to the Corinthians:

> For I delivered to you as of first importance what I also received, that

Christ died for our sins in accordance with the scriptures, that he was buried, that he was raised on the third day in accordance with the scriptures, and that he appeared to Cephas, then to the twelve. Then he appeared to more than five hundred brethren at one time, most of whom are still alive, though some have fallen asleep. Then he appeared to James, then to all the apostles. Last of all, as one untimely born, he appeared also to me. (*1 Cor*. 15: 3-8)

In this same letter Paul stated the essence of the Christian faith.

Now if Christ is preached as raised from the dead, how can some of you say that there is no resurrection of the dead? But if there is no resurrection of the dead, then Christ has not been raised; if Christ has not been raised, then our preaching is in vain and your faith is in vain. (*1 Cor*. 15: 12-14)

Many modern scholars underscore Paul's words and make them the central core of Christian belief. Norman Perrin, for example, in his book *The Resurrection According to Matthew, Mark and Luke* wrote that the information contained in the letters of Paul concerning the resurrection are of vital importance. Perrin selected four quotations from Paul's letters for consideration. They are *1 Cor*. 15: 3-8, *Gal*. 1: 15-16, *1 Cor*. 9: 1-2, *Phil*. 3: 7-11. Each one of these quotations reaffirms the Christian faith that Jesus was resurrected from the dead and the evidence offered is the appearances of Jesus to his followers and especially to the apostle Paul. (Perrin, p.82)

Hans Küng, one of the most famous of contemporary Christian theologians, restates the Christian faith in his book *On Being A Christian*. He maintains that Jesus was a human being who actually died but through the miraculous intervention of God was resurrected from the tomb. Küng argues that the earliest Christological formulas contained in Paul's letters are concentrated on 'Jesus' death and resurrection' (Küng, p.346). Küng argues further that Easter is the 'permanent, constitutive core of the Christian creed', and that the resurrection message is 'central to the Christian faith and at the same time the basis for all further statements of faith' (Küng, p.347).

Tom Harpur, the distinguished New Testament scholar, also follows in the footsteps of Paul. In his book *For Christ's Sake* he contends that 'the faith that Jesus, who was crucified, who died and was buried, was later seen alive by the Apostles and large groups of the disciples is the foundation of Christian belief and life' (Harpur, p.80). Once again the appearances of Jesus to the disciples is the evidence which is given for the resurrection of Jesus.

3

Harpur writes that the unequivocal teaching of the New Testament is that 'Jesus was very much a normal human being. He truly feared death on the cross. He really did die and was buried in the utter helplessness of all humanity. He was raised back to a new dimension and plane... by a miracle of God's mercy and renewing power' (Harpur, p.82).

Dr. Terry L. Miethe, who is Dean of the Oxford Study Centre, Oxford, England, argues that the resurrection is the most important question for the Christian faith. He maintains that the Christian faith exists only 'if Jesus rose from the dead' (Habermas and Flew, xi).

The evidence which is normally given for the 'resurrection' of Jesus are his appearances to Mary Magdalene, the disciples, and the apostle Paul. Later, when this 'evidence' is thoroughly examined, I will argue that his appearances can be explained not by a unique act of God, as posited by the apostle Paul, Hans Küng, Tom Harpur, and Terry Miethe, but by an analysis of the psychological phenomena which can accompany grief and the emotional consequences of conversion disorder. These experiences, in turn, led to dramatic changes in the lives of Mary Magdalene, the disciples, and Paul.

Next, however, I will begin this analysis of the Christian doctrine of the resurrection by reviewing the evidence which is contained in the New Testament.

Chapter 2

The New Testament Evidence for the Resurrection

The New Testament is an exceedingly complicated book which requires some preliminary comments in order to understand the relevant sequence of events and ideas. The Gospels of Matthew, Mark, Luke and John were not written by the disciples or by the close followers of Jesus. The actual authors are unknown and they were not eye-witnesses to any of the events at the tomb. From a contemporary historical perspective the tomb[2] stories are dismissed by some very reliable New Testament scholars. Yet the authors of the Gospel stories, whoever they were, had some previously written material available to them and they also had word-of-mouth traditions with which they were familiar. Thus, there was no simple and accurate source for the writers of the Gospels.

The Gospel accounts were written between forty and seventy years following the death of Jesus, and each Gospel was written for a different audience, thus influencing the way in which each was written. Understanding this timing is essential if we want to make sense of the records. Norman Perrin, the well-known New Testament scholar, wrote that 'the Gospels were not written by eye-witnesses of the ministry of Jesus... and when we speak of "Matthew", "Mark", "Luke", or "John" we do so only for convenience; the actual names of the evangelists are lost to us forever' (Perrin [1982], p.42).

Jesus suffered a common criminal's death by crucifixion. The exact date of this event is unknown, but *The Oxford Dictionary of the Christian Church* suggests 'the years AD 29, 30, or 33...' (Cross and Livingstone, p.737). Most scholars use the year AD 30.

Mark is the earliest Gospel and is dated around AD 70 (Perrin, p.257). Matthew 'was probably written about a generation after Mark, about AD 90' (Perrin, p.264). Luke is dated around AD 85 (Perrin, p.294), and John is dated between AD 90-100 (Perrin, p.341).

5

The *Acts of the Apostles* was written by Luke; thus, the book is often referred to as Luke/Acts. Perrin dates Luke/Acts as of AD 85, 'plus or minus five years' (Perrin [1982], p.294).

Paul's letters were written before the Gospels. Contemporary scholars have attributed seven letters to Paul. They are 1 Thessalonians, 1 Corinthians, 2 Corinthians, Philippians, Philemon, Galatians, and Romans (Perrin, p 43). These letters were all written between the years AD 50-60. Thus, the influence of Paul upon the content of the Gospels must have been considerable since his letters constitute the oldest strata in the New Testament.

In spite of the fact that the Gospels were written after the letters of Paul, I will begin with the Gospel accounts of the events which immediately followed the crucifixion and burial of Jesus. I begin here because it is logical to think of the death and resurrection first and then of Paul because he became involved with the followers of Jesus somewhere between six and eleven years following Jesus' death. Furthermore, most people are familiar with the Easter morning stories since Easter is celebrated around the world. This is the beginning point which is most familiar to the average churchgoer.

The Gospel Accounts of the Resurrection

In the following analysis of the Gospel stories I have made a sharp division between the events on Easter morning and the events which follow later in the day on Easter, and, in some instances, many weeks later. I have made this division because the early morning events centre, almost exclusively, around Mary Magdalene and the other women.

I will consider each Gospel, and even though this may appear to be repetitive and somewhat tedious, it is necessary because it shows the differences among the Gospels and also clarifies all the early morning evidence which is usually cited to prove the resurrection of Jesus.

As I proceed in the close examination of the Gospels, I will show that the records can hardly constitute evidence because of their very nature. Yet, there are no other records to which we can refer. However, if we examine the records closely perhaps something approaching 'evidence' will emerge; but the evidence which emerges will not support the traditional idea of 'resurrection'.

In order to control this examination I will ask and answer six factual questions concerning the Easter morning events as they are presented in each Gospel, and give a brief summary. This method will clarify three important points: 1) What evidence is presented in each Gospel concerning the resurrection? 2) Was there or was there not an actual witness to the physical resurrection of Jesus? By witness I mean someone who actually verified that Jesus was dead and then actually saw him being physically raised from the dead; and 3) What is reported concerning the activities of Mary Magdalene and the disciples immediately following the first appearance of Jesus to Mary Magdalene?

The Easter Morning Events According to Each Gospel

Following the crucifixion of Jesus, Joseph of Arimathea went to Pilate and asked for Jesus' body. Pilate asked the centurion if Jesus was dead and the centurion confirmed the death. Then Pilate gave the body to Joseph. (*Mark* 15: 45)

Joseph wrapped Jesus' body in a linen shroud and then laid it in a tomb which had been hewn out of rock. The tomb was closed by rolling a stone against the door. (*Mark* 15: 46)

1) On the morning of the first day (Easter morning), who went to the tomb?

The principal ones who went to the tomb on the morning of the first day were the women who were the followers of Jesus. According to Mark they were Mary Magdalene and Mary the mother of James. According to Matthew the two Marys went to the tomb where they had a brief encounter with Jesus. In Luke several women went to the tomb. However, John presents the most inclusive report. This record indicates that Mary Magdalene went to the tomb, and when she found the stone rolled away she went and told the disciples.

> Now on the first day of the week Mary Magdalene came to the tomb early, while it was still dark, and saw that the stone had been taken away from the tomb. So she ran, and went to Simon Peter and the other disciple, the one whom Jesus loved, and said to them, 'They have taken the Lord out of the tomb, and we do not know where they have laid him.' Peter came out with the other disciple, and they went toward the tomb. They both ran, but the other disciple outran Peter and reached the tomb first. (*John* 20: 1-4)

2) Why did they go there?

Essentially, the women went to the tomb just to see what was happening, or they went to the tomb in order to anoint the body of Jesus.

7

According to Matthew an angel descended from heaven and rolled back the stone and then announced to the women that Jesus had been raised from the dead and he would meet the disciples in Galilee.

3) Who rolled the stone away?

The stone was either just rolled away or an angel of the Lord rolled the stone away.

4) Did they enter the tomb?

According to Mark the women entered the tomb and were advised by a young man dressed in white that Jesus had been raised from the dead and he would meet the disciples in Galilee. In Matthew there was an angel who invited them into the tomb. According to Luke they were met by two men in dazzling apparel who advised them that Jesus was raised from the dead on the third day in accordance with the scriptures. In John both Peter and the other disciple entered the tomb and they saw cloths lying in the tomb but Jesus was not there. When Mary Magdalene looked into the tomb she saw two angels dressed in white. Mary cried because they had taken Jesus out of the tomb. When Mary turned to leave she encountered an appearance of Jesus:

> When she turned around to leave she saw Jesus but she supposed him to be the gardener. Jesus said to her, 'Woman, why are you weeping? Whom do you seek?' She said, 'Sir if you have carried him away, tell me where you have laid him, and I will take him away.' Jesus said to her, 'Mary.' She said, 'Rabboni!' (Rabboni means teacher, *John* 20: 14-16).

5) Did Mary and the women tell the disciples?

Mark indicates that the women were afraid to tell the disciples. According to Matthew the women ran to tell the disciples. Luke reports that Mary Magdalene and Joanna the mother of James told the disciples but they considered these stories to be idle tales. In John Mary Magdalene told the disciples.

6) Did the women witness a resurrection?

According to Mark the women saw *a young man in the tomb who said that Jesus had been resurrected* and he would meet the disciples in Galilee. According to Matthew *the angel said that Jesus had risen.* Yet, as they turned to leave the tomb they saw an appearance of Jesus.

8

And behold, Jesus met them and said, 'Hail!' And they came up and took hold of his feet and worshipped him. Then Jesus said to them, 'Do not be afraid; go and tell my brethren to go to Galilee, and there they will see me' (*Matt.* 28: 9-10).

Luke writes that many women went to the tomb and while there they encountered two men dressed in dazzling apparel. Also, the women in this account do not see an appearance of Jesus of Nazareth. According to John, Mary saw two angels in the tomb, and she saw an appearance of Jesus of Nazareth and there was a brief conversation between Mary and the appearance of Jesus.

This very brief review of the Easter morning events recorded in the Gospels shows *there was no one who saw an actual event of Jesus being physically resurrected from the dead. Mary Magdalene went to the tomb where she saw appearances of angels, young men, and Jesus. When she told the disciples what she had seen they did not believe her*. However, Peter and the other disciple went to the tomb where they saw cloths which, it is presumed, were left there by the resurrected Christ. In the early morning events *the disciples did not witness either a resurrection or an appearance of Jesus*.

From the Gospel accounts of the morning of the first day it becomes quite clear that there was no witness to the actual physical resurrection on Easter morning. By witness I mean someone who actually verified that Jesus was in fact dead and then was a witness to his being removed from the tomb by non-naturalistic means or by a unilateral act of God. The one thing which the Gospels cannot confirm is the physical (flesh-and-blood) resurrection of Jesus of Nazareth. It does confirm that Mary Magdalene *did see appearances of Jesus following his death.* These appearances will be discussed in the next chapter and I will argue that these appearances were grief-related illusions.

The Post-Easter Morning Appearances to the Disciples According to the Gospel of Mark (AD70)

I have now shown that on Easter morning the disciples did not witness a physical resurrection or experience any appearances of Jesus, and they did not believe the reports which were given to them by Mary Magdalene. We now confront the task of following the activities of the disciples after the Easter morning events.

The Gospel of Mark is a confusing document because modern

scholars now believe that the Gospel originally ended at Chapter 16: 8. This verse is:

> And they [Mary Magdalene and Mary the mother of James] went out and fled from the tomb; for trembling and astonishment had come upon them; and they said nothing to anyone, for they were afraid. (*Mark* 16: 8)

In *The Oxford Annotated Bible: Revised Standard Version* the editors noted that 'modern scholars generally agree that the original text of Mark (as far as we have it) ends abruptly here' (May and Metzger, p.1238). However, in the King James Version of the Gospel of Mark the ending is verse 16: 20. Thus, the verses *Mark* 16: 9-20 were later additions to the text.

If the results of modern scholarship are accepted then there is no record of any post-Easter morning encounters between Jesus and the disciples reported in the Gospel of Mark. It is assumed, however, that the disciples returned to Galilee.

In spite of the above results of modern scholarship it is useful to look at the ending that was added to the text, because it will give us some insight into the thinking of the person or persons who made the addition. *Mark* 16: 9-20 reads:

> Now when he [Jesus] rose early on the first day of the week, he appeared first to Mary Magdalene, from whom he had cast out seven demons. She went out and told those who had been with him, as they mourned and wept. But when they heard that he was alive and had been seen by her, they would not believe it.
>
> After this he appeared in another form to two of them, as they were walking into the country. And they went back and told the rest, but they did not believe them.
>
> Afterward he appeared to the eleven themselves as they sat at table; and he upbraided them for their unbelief and hardness of heart, because they had not believed those who saw him after he had risen. And he said to them, 'Go into all the world and preach the Gospel to the whole creation. He who believes and is baptized will be saved; but he who does not believe will be condemned. And these signs will accompany those who believe: in my name they will cast out demons; they will speak in new tongues; they will pick up serpents, and if they drink any deadly thing, it will not hurt them; they will lay their hands on the sick, and they will recover.'
>
> So then the Lord Jesus, after he had spoken to them, was taken up into heaven, and sat down at the right hand of God. And they went forth and preached everywhere, while the Lord worked with them and

confirmed the message by the signs that attended it. Amen. (*Mark* 16: 9-20)

This addition to the text makes the following points: 1) The resurrected Christ appeared first to Mary Magdalene, and when she reported this to those who had been with Jesus they did not believe her. The reference that Jesus had cast out seven demons from Mary implies that Mary had been ill. 2) Two of the followers of Jesus went for a walk in the country where they saw an appearance of Jesus. When they went back and told the followers of Jesus what they had seen they would not believe them. 3) Later, when the eleven disciples were eating together they saw an appearance of Jesus who upbraided them for not believing what they had been told. Then the person who made the addition to the text gave his version of the signs that would verify belief in the resurrected Christ. Through belief, the disciples would be able to cast out demons, speak in tongues, handle snakes, drink any deadly liquid and not be hurt, and be able to lay on hands for healing the sick. 4) After Jesus had delivered his instructions to the disciples he was taken up to heaven where he sat down at the right hand of God. The disciples then went forth to preach the Gospel.

If *Mark* 16: 9-20 is accepted as being a part of the Gospel of Mark then this account indicates that no one believed Mary Magdalene, and they did not believe the two who went for a walk and saw an appearance of Jesus. The disciples, while eating, arrived at a sense of mission which was attributed to Jesus' appearance before them.

The Post-Easter Morning Appearances to the Disciples According to the Gospel of Matthew (AD90)

The ending of the Gospel of Matthew, as contrasted with Mark, gives some information about the activities of the disciples; however, there continue to be many problems with the account given in Matthew. The ending of Matthew given in *The Oxford Annotated Bible* is:

> Now the eleven disciples went to Galilee, to the mountain to which Jesus directed them. And when they saw him they worshipped him; but some doubted. And Jesus came and said to them, 'All authority in heaven and on earth has been given to me. Go therefore and make disciples of all nations, baptizing them in the name of the Father and of the Son and of the Holy Spirit, teaching them to observe all that I have commanded you; and lo, I am with you always, to the close of the age' (*Matt.* 28: 16-20).

11

The New Testament scholar Tom Harpur wrote as follows concerning the above passage:

> Finally, it is worth commenting on the last two verses of Matthew (28: 19-20). Here alone in the Gospels do we find any reference to the Trinitarian formula. Jesus tells the disciples, 'Go ye therefore, and teach all nations, baptizing them in the name of the Father, and of the Son, and of the Holy Ghost'. All but the most conservative of scholars agree that at least the latter part of this command was inserted later. (Harpur, p.84)

I have shown that the ending in the Gospel of Matthew was changed from the original. Thus, in both Mark and Matthew the endings were changed in order to reflect a later, different point of view.

However, according to Matthew the disciples went to the mountain in Galilee where they 'saw' Jesus, but some of the disciples doubted.

What do we actually have in the Gospel of Matthew? First, the disciples did not witness a physical resurrection of Jesus of Nazareth at the tomb because they fled to Galilee. Second, while they were on the mountain in Galilee one or possibly more of the disciples 'saw' Jesus but some of the disciples doubted. This will be discussed in the next chapter. Third, we have a Gospel in which the ending has been altered. The account in Matthew cannot be used to confirm the actual physical resurrection of Jesus of Nazareth.

The Post-Easter Morning Appearances to the Disciples According to the Gospel of Luke (AD85)

Luke's version is substantially different from Matthew in that he has made three additions to the resurrection narratives. These additions are quite significant and are of great interest.

Luke adds the story that on Easter Sunday two of Jesus' followers were walking on the road to Emmaus. As they walked and talked about the recent events in Jerusalem, Jesus joined them. They did not recognize him until they had arrived home and broke bread together. At the breaking of bread, when they recognized Jesus, he immediately disappeared. These two followers of Jesus returned to Jerusalem to tell the disciples.

> And they rose that same hour and returned to Jerusalem; and they found the eleven gathered together and those who were with them, who said, 'The Lord has risen indeed, and has appeared to Simon!' Then

12

they told what had happened on the road, and how he [Jesus] was known to them in the breaking of the bread. (*Luke* 24: 33-35)

Luke now reports that Jesus appeared to the eleven disciples and all those who were with them. In this appearance Jesus insisted that he was not a spirit and that he was really real. Jesus, in order to prove his reality, took a piece of fish and ate it.

As they were saying this, Jesus himself stood among them. But they were startled and frightened, and supposed that they saw a spirit. And he said to them, 'Why are you troubled, and why do questionings rise in your hearts? See my hands and my feet, that it is I myself; handle me, and see; for a spirit has not flesh and bones as you see that I have.' And while they still disbelieved for joy, and wondered, he said to them, 'Have you anything here to eat?' They gave him a piece of broiled fish, and he took it and ate before them. (*Luke* 24: 36-43)

Following this appearance Jesus led the disciples out as far as Bethany where he blessed them and then parted from them.

Then he [Jesus] led them out as far as Bethany and lifting up his hands he blessed them. While he blessed them, he parted from them. And they returned to Jerusalem with great joy, and were continually in the temple blessing God. (*Luke* 24: 50-53)

Either one of the disciples or someone who was with them said:

The Lord is risen indeed, and has appeared to Simon [Peter]. (*Luke* 24: 34)

Jesus' appearance to Peter was reported by someone in the group.

These additions to the story by the author of Luke are an effort on his part to make some final arguments for the meaning and direction he wanted for Christianity. Luke seems to argue for the flesh-and-blood resurrection of Jesus and he also centred these activities in Bethany and Jerusalem.

The Post-Easter Morning Appearances to the Disciples According to the Gospel of John (AD90-100)

In John, Jesus appears three times to the disciples. The first appearance was in the evening of the first day, or on Easter Sunday. John does not indicate where the disciples held their meeting but it is assumed that it was either in or near Jerusalem. The account of this appearance is as follows:

On the evening of that day, the first day of the week, the doors being shut where the disciples were, for fear of the Jews, Jesus came and

13

stood among them and said to them, 'Peace be with you.' When he had said this he showed them his hands and his side. Then the disciples were glad when they saw the Lord. Jesus said to them again, 'Peace be with you. As the father has sent me, even so I send you.' And when he had said this, he breathed on them, and said to them, 'Receive the Holy Spirit. If you forgive the sins of any, they are forgiven; if you retain the sins of any, they are retained' (*John* 20: 19-23).

When the disciples reported the above encounter with the resurrected Jesus to Thomas he did not believe the disciples.

Now Thomas, one of the twelve, called the Twin, was not with them when Jesus came. So the other disciples told him, 'We have seen the Lord.' But he said to them, 'Unless I see in his hands the print of nails, and place my finger in the mark of the nails, and place my hand in his side I will not believe' (*John* 20: 24-25).

Jesus' second appearance occurred eight days later. John reported:

Eight days later, his disciples were again in the house, and Thomas was with them. The doors were shut but Jesus came and stood among them, and said, 'Peace be with you.' Then he said to Thomas, 'Put your finger here, and see my hands; and put out your hand, and place it in my side; do not be faithless, but believing' (*John* 20: 26-27).

The third appearance was on the beach at the Sea of Tiberias. Norman Perrin suggests that this was a later addition to the text. Perrin writes:

Surely the evangelist intended his Gospel to end at 20: 31, and Chapter 21 has been added as an epilogue by another writer. The language is not quite that of the evangelist; yet the epilogue certainly echoes his concerns... The purpose of the epilogue seems to be ecclesiastical. The author is now concerned with the ongoing life and work of the church in the world and appears to feel that from this viewpoint something needs to be added to the gospel narrative. (Perrin [1982], p.361)

The early morning encounter with the resurrected Christ at the sea of Tiberias is as follows:

After this Jesus revealed himself again to the disciples by the Sea of Tiberias; and he revealed himself in this way. Simon Peter, Thomas called the Twin, Nathanael of Cana in Galilee, the sons of Zebedee, and two others of his disciples were together. Simon Peter said to them, 'I am going fishing.' They said to him, 'We will go with you.' They went out and got into the boat; but that night they caught nothing.

Just as day was breaking, Jesus stood on the beach; yet the disciples did not know that it was Jesus. Jesus said to them, 'Children, have you any fish?' They answered him, 'No.' He said to them, 'Cast the net on the right side of the boat, and you will find some.' So they cast it, and now they were not able to haul it in, for the quantity of fish. That disciple whom Jesus loved said to Peter, 'It is the Lord!' (*John* 21: 4-7).

Following their successful fishing, and having eaten breakfast, there were several verbal exchanges reported between the resurrected Jesus and the disciples.

The Post-Easter Morning Appearances to the Disciples According to the Acts of the Apostles (AD80-90)

At the very beginning of the book of Acts we are introduced to two great turning-points in Christian history. These are the Ascension, which was the day that the resurrected Jesus Christ ascended into heaven and the disciples became apostles, and the Pentecost, which was the moment when the Holy Spirit descended upon the apostles. The Pentecost, however, is not recorded in the Gospels. There are accounts of Ascensions in the Gospels but none are placed in the 40- and 50-day framework as they are in the Acts. This is significant, as we shall see at a later point.

According to the book of Acts, Jesus presented himself to his followers many times over a 40-day period following his death. The women who were following Jesus were present at the time of his Ascension.

> All those with one accord devoted themselves to prayer, together with the women and Mary the mother of Jesus, and with his brothers. (*Acts* 1: 14)

> To them he presented himself alive after his passion by many proofs, appearing to them during forty days, and speaking of the kingdom of God. And while staying with them he charged them not to depart from Jerusalem, but to wait for the promise of the Father, which, he said, 'you heard from me, for John baptized with water, but before many days you will be baptized with the Holy Spirit... But you shall receive power when the Holy Spirit has come upon you; and you shall be my witness in Jerusalem and in all Judea and Samaria and to the end of the earth.' And when he had said this, as they were looking on, he was lifted up, and a cloud took him out of their sight. (*Acts* 1: 3-9)

Thus Jesus told the disciples what they were going to do: to be witness to him 'in Jerusalem and in all Judea and Samaria and to the end of the earth' (*Acts* 1: 8).

15

Ten days later, the day of the Pentecost, the disciples committed themselves to what they would do.

> When the day of the Pentecost had come, they were all together in one place... And they were all filled with the Holy Spirit and began to speak with other tongues, as the spirit gave them utterance... But Peter, standing with the eleven, lifted up his voice and addressed them... Now when they heard this they were cut to the heart, and said to Peter and the rest of the Apostles, 'Brethren, what shall we do?' And Peter said to them, 'Repent, and be baptized every one of you in the name of Jesus Christ and for the forgiveness of your sins; and you shall receive the gift of the Holy Spirit'... And they devoted themselves to the apostles' teaching and fellowship, and to the breaking of bread and the prayers. (*Acts* 2: 1-42, selected quotations)

In the *Acts of the Apostles* the events surrounding the death of Jesus are placed in the format of the Resurrection, the Ascension, and the Pentecost. This is the format of the emergent Christian doctrine which will become very important to us in the next chapter.

The Post-Easter Morning Appearances as presented in Paul's Letters (AD50-60)

The oldest and most important record of the post-Easter appearances is contained in *1 Cor* 15: 3-8. It is now possible to compare the simple and earliest report of the resurrection from Paul with the complicated and confusing reports that are contained in the Gospels. Paul wrote:

> For I delivered to you as of first importance what I also received, that Christ died for our sins in accordance with the scriptures, that he was buried, that he was raised on the third day in accordance with the scriptures, and that he appeared to Cephas, then to the twelve. Then he appeared to more than five hundred brethren at one time, most of whom are still alive, though some have fallen asleep. Then he appeared to James, then to all the apostles. Last of all, as one untimely born, he appeared also to me.

Today, most scholars agree that Paul, in the above quotation, recorded a credal statement concerning Jesus' death and resurrection and that this creed had been used in the early church. Paul wrote that what he delivered to his followers was what he had received. Probably, he received this creed from Peter and James when he visited them in Jerusalem somewhere between eleven and seventeen years following the crucifixion of Jesus. If he received it in Jerusalem then the creed might have been in circulation for some years and it could be dated very close to the actual crucifixion. Thus, this quotation from Paul is believed to contain the earliest information in the New Testament concerning Jesus' death and resurrection. (Habermas and Flew, p.23) Since so much weight is given to this quotation from Paul, I want to see what can be confirmed from the writings which were much later – the Gospels.

We must note Perrin's caution about such a project. He wrote that the appearance stories in Matthew and Luke are difficult to reconcile with *1 Cor.* 15. This is so because the stories recorded in the Gospels were told and retold over a period of thirty years before they were recorded. In addition the intense theological motivation of Matthew and Mark seriously affected the way in which they wrote the stories. (Perrin [1982], p.82)

Even though Perrin cautions us on this point, it is important to make some fundamental distinctions which are necessary to a fuller understanding of the mission and history of the Christian church.

First, the use of the terms the 'twelve' and the 'apostles' in *1 Cor.* 15 must be clarified. In the Gospels it is customary to use these two terms interchangeably. The 'twelve' were the original disciples and would have included Judas. After Judas' suicide they were referred to as the eleven. After Matthias replaced Judas they were referred to, once again, as the twelve.

Thus when Jesus appeared to the 'twelve' and to the 'apostles' (Matthias replaced Judas) he appeared to the same group of people. Later, Paul was deemed to have been an apostle because Jesus appeared to him; yet, Paul was never a disciple.

However, in later Christian history there developed a sharp difference between 'disciples' and 'apostles'. The disciples were those who worked with the man Jesus of Nazareth and they were with him up to his crucifixion. Apostles, however, were those who had witnessed the resurrected Christ and such witnessing could only occur following the death of Jesus. Thus, those disciples who 'witnessed' the resurrected Christ became apostles. The term apostle was then enlarged to make room for Paul who was never a disciple but he, after 'witnessing' the resurrected Christ on the road to Damascus, became an apostle. Harvey Cox writes that the mission of the church begins with those who met with the risen Christ, the apostles, and not with the disciples. Therefore the church did not trace itself back to the historical Jesus (Cox, p.150). In effect the Christian church anchored itself primarily in the Christ of faith and then gave secondary importance to the man Jesus. This is the significance of the distinction between 'disciples' and 'apostles'.

According to *1 Cor.* 15, the first person to whom Jesus appeared was Cephas or Peter. Again Peter was one of the disciples. However, was there a special appearance to him separate from the other disciples? There is only one reference to this separate appearance and this is in the Gospel of Luke. When the two followers of Jesus returned to Jerusalem from Emmaus they joined the eleven. Luke wrote:

> There they found the eleven and the rest of the company had assembled, and were saying, 'It is true: the Lord has risen; he has appeared to Simon [Peter]...' (Luke 24: 34).

Paul then reports that Jesus appeared to the five hundred. This is the only reference in the New Testament to an appearance to the five hundred.

The distinguished Anglican Bishop Barnes in his book *The Rise of Christianity* concluded that the appearance to five hundred could not have been historical. He wrote that the appearance to 'above five hundred at once' would have been 'of such overwhelming value as a piece of evidence for the resurrection that it would have been in the forefront of Christian apologetic.' However, there is no hint of it in Matthew, Luke or John. Barnes concluded that this incident could not have been historical and that it was a later addition to the text. (Barnes, p.173)

Following Jesus' appearance to five hundred, Paul wrote that Jesus appeared to James, who was Jesus' brother. Once again there is no reference in the Gospels to any appearance to James. (Cross and Livingstone, p.722)

Finally, Paul reports the appearance of Jesus to himself.

From this very careful analysis of the Gospels, the Acts of the Apostles, and the letters of Paul we can draw some preliminary conclusions concerning the appearances of Jesus to the disciples and others.

In essence this is what the New Testament presents: a) Jesus died on the cross; b) there was no witness to the actual physical resurrection of Jesus of Nazareth; c) the women who went to the tomb on Easter morning, especially Mary Magdalene, saw what they deemed to be appearances of Jesus; d) on Easter morning the disciples did not believe Mary Magdalene's report that she had seen Jesus so they fled to Galilee or to Jerusalem depending on which Gospel you read; e) the mental state of the disciples and others following the death of

Jesus was one of trying to make up their minds as to what they should do now that Jesus was dead. The disciples also saw what they believed were appearances of Jesus.

Contradictions in Hans Küng's Theory of the Resurrection

The above facts are well known to Christian scholars, but the scholars who argue for the resurrection usually shift their argument from the evidence for the resurrection to the disciples' belief in the resurrection. *Many Christian theologians argue that if the disciples believed that Jesus was resurrected, then the resurrection must have occurred.* Hans Küng, for example, wrote:

> A close analysis of the Easter accounts reveals insuperable discrepancies and inconsistencies... *There is no evidence of a resurrection.* There is no one in the whole New Testament who claims to have been a witness to the resurrection. (Küng, p.347, my italics)

Küng then shifts the ground in the following words:

> At the same time it becomes clear that anyhow, the when or where of the narratives is of secondary importance by comparison with the fact – of which there is no doubt in the different sources – of the resurrection, which in every context is clearly not identical with death and burial. (Küng, p.348)

Küng then maintains that because the disciples saw appearances of Jesus they believed that the resurrection had actually occurred. Küng concludes that the resurrection is an historical fact because the disciples had faith that the resurrection actually occurred.

This is the substance of Küng's argument for the resurrection, and his explanations lead him into insurmountable difficulties.

> Today we speak perhaps too glibly of 'resurrection' in the sense simply of Jesus' action and his power. In the New Testament however 'resurrection' is rightly understood as 'raising by God.' It is essentially a work of God on Jesus... (Küng, p.349).

Küng argues that the resurrection is a unique unilateral action of God upon the dead body of Jesus of Nazareth.

> The fact that God intervenes... at the point where everything is at an end from the human point of view, this... despite the maintenance of natural law... is the true miracle of the resurrection: the miracle of the beginning of a new life out of death. (Küng, p.350)

This is Küng's insurmountable difficulty: on the one hand, he argues that God must maintain natural law but, on the other hand, that in this one instance in human history God defied natural law and resurrected Jesus from the tomb.

Thus Küng must maintain that a miracle has occurred through the hands of God even though in explaining his concept of God he wrote:

> The present-day understanding of God presupposes the modern scientific explanation of the world: weather and victories in battle, illness and cures... are no longer explained by the direct intervention of God, but by natural causes. (Küng, p.81)

Yet, with regard to the resurrection, Küng asserts that it was a true miracle in that life came out of death in the literal sense. Here Küng uses an agricultural metaphor; plant a seed, it dies and new life comes from the seed. The body is the seed and when planted new life of a radically different kind emerges from the seed.

The problem with the agricultural metaphor is the assumption that a dead body was a seed. It is true that the death of a prophet may inspire renewed commitment in his or her followers but to maintain that a dead body was actually resurrected by a unilateral act of God, and to offer as proof the conflicting 'evidence' as presented in the New Testament, is a major historical error. This is especially important because Küng himself argues that there is no evidence of a resurrection in the New Testament.

The Gospel accounts of the Easter morning events at the tomb are inconsistent, contradictory, and inconclusive. The reports of appearances to Mary Magdalene, the other women, the disciples, the wider community, and the apostle Paul do not constitute proof for physical resurrection when there was no witness to the actual physical resurrection of Jesus of Nazareth. In the next chapter I will argue that Mary Magdalene and the disciples did see what they believed were 'appearances' of Jesus but those 'appearances' were grief-related hallucinations or illusions. It must be understood, however, that in current grief literature such grief-related hallucinations are generally considered to be helpful accompaniments of grief.

Chapter 3

Bereavement and the Myth of the Resurrection, the Ascension and the Pentecost

The New Testament records offer no support for the classical Christian arguments for the resurrection of Jesus of Nazareth because there was no witness to his physical resurrection. Yet, we are left with the evidence that the followers of Jesus, Mary Magdalene and the disciples saw appearances[3] of Jesus, and that these appearances led to the emergence of their faith in Jesus' 'physical resurrection'.

I offer a new hypothesis concerning the 'appearances' of Jesus to his followers. The hypothesis is that the followers of Jesus experienced grief-related hallucinations or illusions following the traumatic death of their leader. By hallucination I mean having a sensory experience of something that does not exist outside the mind. Such hallucinations can be manifested as visual, auditory, or illusory experiences. What is new in the approach which I am taking is the fact that hallucinations[4] can be a normal accompaniment of grief. When the Gospel records are approached with this simple and plausible hypothesis we will be able to identify the emotional ground which can normally and naturally give rise to appearances, and appreciate how the followers of Jesus developed a religious point of view that was in keeping with their understanding of their very real experiences.

However, in order to comprehend the relationship between grief and the emotional experiences of the followers of Jesus it is necessary to do some preliminary work. It is important to understand: 1) the role and psychological significance of a prophet; and 2) the normal psychological ground out of which appearances or apparitions and other illusions emerge.

21

The Role and Psychological Significance of a Prophet

Jesus of Nazareth was a charismatic personality and a prophet, and he was in the tradition of the Old Testament prophets even though his message was considerably different from the older prophets.

Jesus thought of himself as a prophet. When he taught in his own synagogue in Nazareth the people were astonished at his teachings. In fact they became angry with him because he was 'only' the son of the local carpenter. Jesus said:

> A prophet is honoured everywhere except in his own country, and among his own people. (*Matt.* 13: 57)

When Jesus was in Jerusalem at the time of the Passover, he was welcomed by the people and they believed that he was a prophet. As he entered the city, all the people were in agitation: 'Who is this?' they asked. The crowd replied, 'This is the prophet Jesus from Nazareth in Galilee' (*Matt.* 21: 11).

Roger O'Toole, writing in his book *Religion: Classic Sociological Approaches*, discusses the role of a charismatic leader or a prophet. A prophet, through the sheer force of his own personality, is able to challenge the social institutions of his own time. A successful prophet will develop a following from among his own people.

A prophet claims moral authority, in whatever terms it is expressed, and those terms might include divine will. 'The prophet is one who feels himself to be reborn. He is qualitatively different from other men in that he is in touch with or the instrument of a source of authority higher than any which is established' (O'Toole, p.163).

The psychology of the role of a prophet is complex. A prophet becomes a charismatic leader because the leader personifies and is able to speak to the deeper feelings, hopes and aspirations of the average person. When the prophet does this the people transfer a deep level of themselves to the prophet. This transference is both conscious and unconscious. The importance of *healthy* transference cannot be overestimated. Dr Ernest Becker, who was one of the most distinguished cultural anthropologists of our century, published his Pulitzer Prize-winning book *The Denial of Death* in 1973. Transference, according to Becker, *is a necessary ingredient for growth and self-fulfilment*. Becker wrote:

> If transference represents the natural heroic striving for a beyond that gives self-validation and if people need this validation in order to live,

then the psychoanalytic view of transference as simply unreal projection is destroyed. *Projection is necessary and desirable for self-
fulfilment. Otherwise man is overwhelmed by his loneliness and
separation and negated by the very burden of his own life...* projection
is A NECESSARY UNBURDENING of the individual; man cannot live
closed in upon himself and for himself. He must project the meaning
of his life outward, the reason for it, even the blame for it... Technically
we say that transference is a distortion of reality. But now we see that
this distortion has two dimensions: ...distortion due to the fear of life
and death and distortion due to the heroic attempt to assure self-
expansion and the intimate connection of one's inner self to surrounding nature. (Becker, p.158, my italics)

Dr Michael Hill, in his book *A Sociology of Religion*, suggests that
the authority of the prophet grows only to the extent to which people
develop 'personal trust' in the charismatic leader. (Hill, p.147)

In modern times, Dr Martin Luther King was a prophet. Those who
followed King in the late 1960s sincerely and passionately believed
that King would lead American society to a new level of social justice, and would bring peace, equality in race relations and a deeper
understanding and acceptance between blacks and whites in American
society.

Millions of people at all levels of society identified with King. As
people increased their commitment to King's ideals and hopes they
gradually left their old ways of thinking and began to venture forth
with new ideas on race relations and peace.

Those who marched and worked with King made a positive
transference because he was the embodiment of their hopes and
aspirations. Through King's inspiration thousands of average people
confronted prejudice and rigid social structures; consequently, hundreds of thousands of people began to think in new ways. None of
this would have occurred had not King been a prophet with charisma. When people project their deepest hopes and desires upon the
prophet, through transference or trust, that prophet is the walking
embodiment of hope to every person who has made the transference.
When the prophet dies suddenly or is executed or murdered the
followers of the prophet are thrown into severe grief because there
is an abrupt breaking of very important transferences. The task of the
living, then, is to recover from the abrupt loss of their leader by with-
drawing their transferences, and then to carry a part of the load which
was projected externally onto the prophet.

The sudden and traumatic death of a prophet is the catalyst which leads some of the prophet's followers to re-evaluate their lives and in many instances some people change their direction. This deep and profound change revolves around the transferences which were projected onto the prophet. The deeper psychological base for what occurs was identified by Paul Tillich. Ernest Becker wrote:

> Tillich means that man has to have the 'courage to be' himself, to stand on his own two feet, to face up to the external contradictions of the real world... a creature who takes more of the world into himself and develops new forms of courage and endurance. (Becker, p.279)

I have personally witnessed and read about several people who changed their life direction following the death of Dr King. These instances are not part of a systematic study but they are important in their own right. Also, the people involved were not personally close to King but felt close to him because he spoke to their situations as human beings.

On April 6, 1986 Arthur Mitchell appeared on *60 MINUTES* where he was interviewed by Ed Bradley. Arthur Mitchell is the founder and director of the world famous 'Dance Theatre Of Harlem'.

What is of interest is the way in which the Dance Theatre was formed. The key parts of the interview from *60 MINUTES* are:

ED BRADLEY: The Dance Theatre Of Harlem – it all started 16 years ago with the idea of one man to get some of the kids off the streets of Harlem... Then, in 1968, on the verge of leaving for Brazil to help establish a national ballet company there, he heard the news that would change the direction of his life.

> DOUGLAS EDWARDS (on news broadcast): Civil Rights leader Dr Martin Luther King, Jr. was shot at a downtown Memphis hotel shortly before 7:00pm.

MITCHELL: I was going to the airport to catch my flight to Brazil, and they announced that he passed away on the way to the hospital. (Dr King was murdered on April 4, 1968) And I started crying, and I got upset, and I said, 'God damn it!' I said, 'Here again it's happened.' And, so, I just felt that, in my own small way, the best thing for me to do is go do whatever I can do and carry on what-ever I – – and since I believed in what the man was about, carry on the best way I could.

BRADLEY: And what you knew was dance?

MITCHELL: And go back and teach it to young people, and give them a sense of discipline and education in their lives.

BRADLEY: Arthur Mitchell started in Harlem with a handful of students in a converted garage. Sixteen years later, he's still there, but now in a building that houses both the company and a school of 350 students.

Arthur Mitchell had identified with the work of Dr King and he believed in what King was doing for the black people in the United States. When King was murdered, I believe Mitchell withdrew his projections from him and began to take responsibility for the development of his own people in Harlem. Within a couple months following the death of Dr King, Arthur Mitchell opened The Dance Theatre Of Harlem. This is an example of the incredible power of grief following the death of a prophet.

This profound transformation was also exemplified by a black man who belonged to the First Unitarian Church of Chicago where I served as minister from 1963 to 1968. He was a university graduate who was earning his living as a loans officer in a bank. He had an excellent job but his work did not address his internal sense of meaninglessness. As a black person he had experienced the pain of discrimination as it exists in American society and there was no way for him to develop a social response to his anxiety.

When Martin Luther King began the Southern Christian Leadership Conference this very capable and well-trained bank officer began to identify with the hopes and aspirations of black Americans as they were spoken about by Dr King. On weekends he began his first tentative steps to protest discrimination against blacks in Chicago. This discrimination extended into every aspect of life. Blacks could not join labour unions, they were discriminated against in housing, they were harassed and sometimes murdered by the police, their living conditions were substandard, their public education system was second-rate, and the political structure was not responsive to the needs of the black community.

Day after day, week after week, month after month, and year after year this man lived a double life. On the one hand he did his regular job but in his spare time he lived in the world of hope, aspiration, and commitment. In a sense he became accustomed to the dream of equality, to the ideal of a responsive political system, to a better educational system for all blacks, to fair employment for all citizens, and to the dream of peace.

It was not surprising that Dr Martin Luther King's speech in

Washington, D.C. in 1963 was I HAVE A DREAM. This man had become accustomed, in his alternate way of life, to calling for a new level of social justice in American society. The point, however, was this: this commitment, this new level of activity by this person came into being under the inspiration of a charismatic leader – Dr Martin Luther King.

When Dr King was murdered this black man had already projected himself into a new realm of being. When he realized that Dr King was dead he withdrew his transferences from King, resigned his job at the bank, and returned to the university where he majored in Black History. Today, he is a distinguished Professor of Black History in one of America's major universities.

At the First Unitarian Church of Chicago, in the weeks following the death of Dr Martin Luther King, many people came into my office and said, 'Since King died for the garbage workers in Memphis, Tennessee, I must do something for our people.' In one instance a black professor at the University of Chicago resigned and went to teach at the black University in Washington D.C. – Howard University.

Many people re-evaluated their lives and changed their life work as a result of the death of Dr Martin Luther King. In a psychological sense these people grappled with Dr King, as though he was still alive, until they made up their own minds as to the way in which they would redirect their lives.

A black lady whom I knew very well resigned from the University of Chicago Hospital where she worked as a psychiatric social worker and took a job teaching in a black High School as a result of the death of Dr King.

It is very clear that the disciples, after their experiences with Jesus, could not go back to their old profession of being fishermen. They, too, had projected themselves into a new way of life while they were followers of Jesus, and after Jesus' traumatic death the disciples changed their way of life and became teachers and evangelists. The disciples struggled over a 50-day period before they made up their minds as to what they were going to do. I personally observed a similarity between the grieving period of the disciples and the grieving period of the followers of Dr King.

We have already discussed the distinction which is made in Christian theology between disciples and apostles. Perhaps there is a fertile insight into the psychological realities behind this distinction.

26

As long as the disciples were followers of a prophet they were learning and developing their own talents as disciples. However, when the prophet was dead the disciples had to make a psychological transition from being followers to being leaders. That is, they had to take on a new level of responsibility. This happened to Arthur Mitchell and to thousands of followers of Dr King, and this also happened to the followers of Jesus of Nazareth.

Hallucinations as a Normal Psychological Symptom of Grief

Before examining the specific studies on the relationship between grief and hallucinations I want to consider some general statements concerning grief.

An important assumption of this book is that the grief experiences of Mary Magdalene and the disciples were not essentially different from the grief experiences which people have today.

The question of the validity of the assumption that we can generalize from today's grief experiences was the concern of the distinguished anthropologist Dr Paul G Rosenblatt in his book *Grief and Mourning in Cross-Cultural Perspective*. He wanted to know to what extent he and his researchers could generalize from mourning customs and grief behaviour in America. He concluded that it was safe to generalize from the experiences of people in the United States. He wrote:

> In this study of seventy-eight world cultures it seems that American practices and behaviours are a relatively safe base from which to generalize about the species. (Rosenblatt, p.124)

Rosenblatt gives the following definitions of grief, mourning and bereavement, and these definitions will be used throughout this book.

> By GRIEF we mean the sorrow, mental distress, emotional agitation, sadness, suffering, and related feelings caused by death. By MOURNING we mean culturally defined acts that are usually performed when death occurs. The mourning period is the culturally defined time or typical period of time during which these acts of mourning are conventionally performed. By BEREAVEMENT we mean both the period of time following a death, during which grief occurs, and also the state of experiencing grief. (Rosenblatt, p.2)

Rosenblatt indicates that those who are grieving will usually go through three stages in their grieving process. It must be noted,

27

however, that in this study Rosenblatt did not make an inquiry into hallucinations which might possibly accompany grief.

STAGE 1. THE SHOCK OF SUDDEN SEPARATION
Sadness, Anger, Numbness, and Loneliness.

STAGE 2. ACUTE GRIEF
Anger, Fear, Anxiety, Guilt, Denial and General Tension.
Behaviour changes: Loss of appetite, weight loss,·disruption
of work activities, loss of interest, decrease in sociability,
disrupted sleep, disturbing dreams. These symptoms can be
expected to be greater when the death is unexpected.

STAGE 3. WORKING THROUGH
Acceptance of loss, extinction of no longer adaptive
behavioural dispositions, acquisition of new behavioural
dispositions and relationships, dissipation of guilt, anger,
and other disruptive emotions. Finally, arriving at a
state of non-bereavement. (Rosenblatt, pp.6-8)

We will now turn from general statements concerning grief to recent studies which have been devised to show the relationship between grief and hallucinations.

Dr W Dewi Rees, a General Practitioner in England, reported, in the *British Medical Journal* on October 2, 1971, the results of a survey made of both widows and widowers with regard to hallucinations following the death of a spouse. The results of this study are especially interesting.

Dr Rees identified five different kinds of hallucinations experienced by both widows and widowers. They are: 1) feeling the internal presence of the deceased (Illusion); 2) seeing and talking to the deceased (Apparition); 3) hearing the deceased (Auditory); 4) feeling the external presence of the deceased (Illusion); 5) touching or being touched by the deceased (Illusion). I shall refer to these five types of hallucinations as grief-related hallucinations or as core grief hallucinations.

Dr Rees established excellent criteria for accepting an hallucinatory experience. He wrote:

Particular care was taken in assessing the statements of those who reported hallucinatory experiences. Only those who did not rationalize the experience – for instance, by saying that they had seen the deceased 'in their mind's eye' – were listed as being hallucinated. If there was any doubt about the reality of the experience a nil response was recorded. Experiences occurring in bed at night, other than those occurring immediately after retirement, were discounted and recorded as dreams. (Rees, p.38)

In this study 227 widows and 66 widowers were interviewed and about 50% of the women and men said that they experienced hallucinations of their deceased spouses following the death of the spouse. The types of hallucinations were quite varied. Dr Rees wrote:

> For simplification and except where otherwise specifically stated the word 'hallucination' is used to include all hallucinations and illusions. Of the 293 people interviewed 137 (46.7%) had post-bereavement hallucinations. These hallucinations often lasted many years, and at the time of interview 106 (36.1%) people still had hallucinations. The proportions of hallucinated men and women were similar, with 33 (50%) men and 104 (45.8%) women having had hallucinations. The most common type of hallucination is the illusion of feeling the presence of the dead spouse (39.2%). The incidence of the various hallucinations [is]... Auditory hallucinations (13.3%) are slightly less common than visual hallucinations (14.0%), and more than one person in ten has spoken to the dead spouse. The least common hallucination is the feeling of being touched by the dead spouse (2.7%). (Rees, p.38)

It is not necessary for us to go into the details of this study. Yet this study is important because grief is a natural psychological ground for hallucinations and illusions following the death of a spouse or of someone who was especially loved. Rees wrote:

> These hallucinations are considered to be normal and helpful accompaniments of widowhood. (Rees, p.37, my italics)

The widowed people in Rees' study experienced their hallucinations as the result of rather normal deaths. The followers of Jesus, however, watched their leader suffer an agonizing death on a cross. Thus, it is safe to assume that their bereavement experiences might have been more intense than the bereavement experiences of the widows and widowers whose spouses experienced normal deaths. It must be noted that in the New Testament five types of grief-related hallucinations are clearly exhibited or can be inferred – feeling the internal presence of the deceased, feeling the external presence of the deceased, seeing an appearance of the deceased, talking to an apparition of the deceased, and touching the deceased. Obviously, there is no way to actually verify some types of hallucinations, but as we follow event after event following the death of Jesus, something like an educated guess will begin to emerge.

29

Dr Stephen R Shuchter, a psychiatrist on the faculty of the University of California School of Medicine in San Diego, is one of North America's leading authorities on spousal bereavement. In his book *Dimensions of Grief* he has written about the newly bereaved's drive to retrieve the presence of the deceased. He wrote:

> The mind and body of the newly bereaved are so driven to retrieve the loved one who has died that most people, *during the early weeks and months of bereavement, have experiences where they believe they have seen, heard, touched, smelled, or felt the presence of their spouses.* They may be aware that what they are experiencing is an illusion or hallucination, but that does not detract from the 'realness' of the sensation. *The contact takes different forms: searching and waiting for the loved one, experiencing external sensory evidence of his presence, or sensing his presence from within. In other instances the bereaved may talk or write to their dead spouses.* (Shuchter, p.118, my italics)

> Mental health professionals – psychiatrists, psychologists, social workers, nurses, and others – are well aware that people suffering from mental and emotional disorders frequently distort reality and thereby create illusions or hallucinations. In most circumstances these clinical phenomena are considered clear-cut manifestations of mental and emotional illness. *Bereavement is probably the only common experience where these 'symptoms' are not considered particularly pathological. On the one hand, they are distortions of reality and evidence of disordered thinking. On the other hand, in the context of the mental and emotional turmoil of bereavement, they are considered 'normal' experiences – regular and normative (statistically) occurrences among 'normal' people undergoing enormous stress.* (Shuchter, p.119, my italics)

Shuchter then cites case studies from his practice and he identifies each type of hallucination.

The following excerpt about one of his patients, Amalia, identifies the experiences of feeling the presence of her deceased husband and also hearing him open the refrigerator:

> Amalia frequently felt her husband's presence: 'I feel him covering me.' At night she was frightened and had her children sleep in her bedroom. 'I hear him opening the refrigerator at night like he always did' (Shuchter, p.120).

Regarding another case from his practice Shuchter reported that his patient, Marie, saw her deceased husband walk into her bedroom and they had a brief conversation with one another. This exchange was so real that Marie could easily have believed that her husband was actually alive. In this case Marie experienced an apparition of her husband and the apparition talked to her and she responded to the apparition. At this point the apparition was so real to Marie that it could have been considered to have been an appearance. Shuchter wrote:

> Before Oscar died, he had a collection of coins to be given to his children. One night Marie woke to find Oscar in the room putting away the coins. 'I'll tell you, Dr. Shuchter, if I didn't know he was dead, I'd swear to God he was very much alive. It seemed to me he walked in the bedroom and stood in the bedroom door. I looked up and I saw him standing in the door, and he was reaching up like onto this place to get the lighter fluid for his lighter. He looked at me and said, "Don't worry, I'm just going to lock it up in the desk." I said, "A lot of people come in here." Then one of my kids said, "Mom, who are you talking to?" Now that's just how much alive he looked to me' (Shuchter p.120).

Another aspect of grieving can be the constant searching for the deceased on the street or in crowds especially when the living has not, as yet, accepted the death of a spouse. Again Shuchter wrote:

> Earl: 'A lot of time, if I'm watching the crowds at a football game or a baseball game, a person looks like her and the crowd is just passing by pretty swiftly, but I know it isn't her, but it's a person that looks like her' (Shuchter, p.119).

Dr Shuchter also reports instances when the living experience being touched by the deceased. These hallucinations seem to be very, very real.

> After Tom's death Pamela had to go to the hospital for surgery. Following the surgery she realized that she had no husband to take her home and care for her. 'It was one of the most horrible feelings of my life... Then at one point in the afternoon, it was like somebody was touching my head and patting me on the shoulder. I opened my eyes and there was nobody there. I had been thinking about him, you know, how always before if I had been ill, there was always him when I came home. And I just felt like he was there, telling me everything was going to be all right. (Shuchter, p.120-121)

Under the extreme stress of grief the human psyche sometimes works desperately to keep the deceased psychologically alive. The above examples include instances of 1) feeling the presence of the deceased; 2) hearing the deceased; 3) seeing appearances of the deceased; 4) engaging in a conversation with an apparition of the

31

deceased; and 5) being touched by the deceased. In contemporary grief literature these hallucinations are considered to be quite normal since they are a part of the process of coping with the death of a person who was dearly loved.

Grief and the Appearances of Jesus on Easter Morning

My purpose at this point is to show the similarities and the differences between the appearances or apparitions experienced by Mary Magdalene and those experienced by women today. I shall use the words appearance and apparition as synonyms because both can mean instances when something is seen but has no mind-independent physical reality. This is especially so when something is seen and then suddenly disappears.

According to the Gospel of John, Mary Magdalene's first apparition was of two angels in the tomb. One was standing at the head and one was standing at the feet where Jesus had been laid. Today the modern mind does not think about angels; however, the modern mind also knows that apparitions or hallucinations can occur. The subject of angels is very interesting and it is an extensive subject in its own right, but it is germane to the issue of the 'resurrection' of Jesus only to the extent that angels reported that Jesus was resurrected. However, the evidence usually cited for Jesus' resurrection are the appearances.

As Mary turned to leave the tomb she saw an appearance of Jesus. As we have already noted, the account in John is as follows:

> Saying this, she turned around and saw Jesus standing, but she did not know that it was Jesus. Jesus said to her, 'Woman, why are you weeping? Whom do you seek?' Supposing him to be the gardener, she said to him, 'Sir, if you have carried him away, tell me where you have laid him, and I will take him away.' Jesus said to her, 'Mary.' She turned and said to him in Hebrew, 'Rabboni!' (*John* 20: 14-16)

When Mary Magdalene's and Marie's encounters are compared with one another the similarities are indeed striking. The content, however, is quite different.

As Marie 'saw' Oscar, Mary 'saw' Jesus. As Oscar 'spoke' to Marie, Jesus 'spoke' to Mary. As Marie 'spoke' to Oscar, Mary 'spoke' to Jesus. As Oscar suddenly disappeared, Jesus suddenly disappeared.

I maintain that Mary Magdalene's seeing an appearance of Jesus at the tomb constitutes evidence for grief and not for the 'physical resurrection' of Jesus of Nazareth.

Grief and the Apparitions of Jesus to the Disciples following Easter Morning

The original Gospel of Mark reports no appearances or apparitions of Jesus to the disciples.

In the Gospel of Matthew the account of the appearance of Jesus is very brief:

> Now the eleven disciples went to Galilee, to the mountain to which Jesus directed them. And when they saw him they worshipped him; but some doubted. (*Matt.* 28: 16-17)

It is impossible for us to know what the word 'saw' actually meant in this context. This is the case because there are at least five different kinds of hallucinations which the disciples could have experienced and it is impossible to give more than a thoughtful guess. In previous theories of hallucinatory experiences it was always assumed that there was only one kind of hallucination and it could only be seen by one person. In today's research there are five types of hallucinations which are common.

It is clear from the text that the disciples were not in agreement on this occasion. Some of the disciples 'saw' him and others did not. The original Greek word for 'saw' could easily have been translated into English with the word 'experience'. If we accept both translations then the possibilities of the quotation become somewhat clearer.

There are three possibilities. One possibility is that one or more of the disciples saw appearances of the deceased Jesus and attempted to convince the rest of the disciples that they 'saw' him or 'experienced' him. If this was the case, since individual apparitions can only be seen individually, then some experienced him and others did not. The second possibility is that some of the disciples felt the presence of the crucified Jesus. Thus, some would have experienced him and others would not have experienced him. Of course this would not have been an either or situation. Third, there could have been a combination of these two types of hallucinations. Nevertheless, some of the disciples doubted.

Yet, we know from contemporary grief research that feeling the presence of the deceased is the most common grief experience. Dr Shuchter wrote:

Sensing the presence of one's deceased spouse occurs even more frequently without externally perceived stimuli, where the source remains wholly within the bereaved. At times the person has a fairly clear understanding of the forces at work.

MELINDA: 'I know, I have acknowledged that I will not accept his loss, and the way I make up for that, I just feel like he's with me, he's got to be. Because we were so close and you can't lose someone like that. It's a hard thing because I'm a realist, too. Obviously I know he's not with me, but he and I were very close' (Shuchter, p.121).

Whether some of the disciples saw appearances of the deceased Jesus or they simply felt the presence of Jesus will never be known. Yet, we now know that such experiences are a common part of normal grief and cannot be used as evidence for actual physical resurrection.

In the Gospel of Luke the story becomes even more complicated, and when this Gospel is carefully examined from the perspective of grief rather than physical resurrection it takes on a new meaning. It must be repeated, however, that the newly bereaved often desperately search for a continuing contact with the deceased, no matter where they go. Dr Shuchter wrote:

There are many myths about bereavement and the tasks of the grieving spouse. Prevalent in our culture and fostered by the mental health professions is a concept that the bereaved learn to accept the loss and put it behind them, that they 'let go', release the dead, so that they can go on living. The physical facts are that people have no choice but to follow this course of action: the dead are dead, they are buried, and the living continue to live and cope. Emotional realities, however, are far different. Human attachment bonds are established and maintained at emotional levels so deep that the mere fact of physical death cannot truly disrupt these bonds. Our biological and psychological apparatus will not permit it... *An important component of any concept of 'recovery' from grief must of necessity include a true emotional recovery of the lost person.* (Shuchter, p.116, my italics)

Two of Jesus' followers were walking on the road to Emmaus and as they walked they were reviewing the events which had occurred over the last few days in Jerusalem. As they walked Jesus 'joined' them but they did not recognize him until they arrived home. While eating they suddenly recognized Jesus and then Jesus suddenly disappeared. The sudden appearance and disappearance of Jesus indicates that the 'appearance' was a grief-related apparition.

Dr Shuchter reported that Earl, his patient, would search desperately for his deceased wife at football and baseball games. Perhaps the followers of Jesus sensed Jesus' presence and it was as though Jesus was with them on the road. We will never know what actually happened but it is perfectly normal for the grieving to search for and 'see' the deceased on the street and at public events.

A friend of mine who is a retired teacher told me that in the first month following the death of her mother, which was a great loss, everywhere she walked on the street she would see apparitions of her mother. She lived in a small town and she had many memories of walking around the town with her mother when she was a child. She told me that if she had not known that her mother was dead she would have believed that her mother was alive and walking with her.

In accordance with contemporary grief theory it would not have been unusual for some of the followers of Jesus to have seen appearances of Jesus on the road to Emmaus.

When these two followers of Jesus returned to Jerusalem they met with the eleven in a room and were told that Jesus had appeared to Simon.

The author of Luke also reports that Jesus appeared to the eleven and ate a piece of fish.

This story could have been built on an illusion of the presence of Jesus but it is quite certain that by AD85 the stories were exaggerated and changed to meet the needs of the authors of the book. The core grief experience in this gathering could have been feeling the presence of the deceased, and perhaps one or more may have actually seen an apparition of Jesus. Certainly there must have been some core grief experience that was embellished.

Yet it now becomes quite clear that by AD85 the core grief hallucinations were being magnified and altered and used as arguments for the physical rather than the spiritual reality of the 'resurrected' Christ. On the one hand, the evangelists wanted to avoid presenting Jesus as a human being or a prophet (Ebionism), and on the other hand they wanted to avoid his being presented as a disembodied spirit (Docetism).

Norman Perrin addresses this issue in his book *The Resurrection According to Matthew, Mark and Luke*. He wrote:

> In Luke the problem was that in the Hellenistic Greek world it was widely assumed that a religious hero overcame death by being transformed into a spiritual being who no longer had any contact with the essentially unreal world of flesh, blood, and bodies. The Hellenistic Greek world would readily have acclaimed the resurrection of Jesus

as an escape from the world of flesh, blood, and bodies into the world of disembodied spirit, and Jesus would thereby have joined a pantheon of religious heroes in which there was always room for one more. But the evangelist Luke, or the community from which he writes, resisted this tendency to assimilate Jesus into a pantheon of Hellenistic Greek religious heroes by developing an apologetic legend of the corporeality of Jesus as risen. Jesus as risen is not a disembodied spiritual being: he can be seen, touched, and handled; he eats a piece of broiled fish. As in the case of the Matthean apologetic legend, this is also not a narrative that is addressed to a question that is real to us. Our acceptance or rejection of the claim 'Jesus is risen!' will not be determined by a legend concerning the corporeality of his presence as he appeared to his disciples. (Perrin, pp.66-67)

We can guess that the author of Luke/Acts used the core grief hallucinations to argue that the resurrected Jesus was not just a spirit in the Greek sense. The resurrected Jesus was flesh and blood.

The Gospel of John was written between sixty and seventy years following the death of Jesus, and by now this Gospel account had become thoroughly theological with regard to the resurrected Christ. This new story includes a cosmic view of Christ as an agent of God.

It is important to identify this new story because it will allow us to understand why the core grief experiences of the disciples were changed to emphasize the 'physical' reality of the 'resurrected' Christ.

The Gospel of John begins with a theological statement:

In the beginning was the Word, and the Word was with God, and the Word was God. He was in the beginning with God; all things were made through him, and without him was not anything made that was made. (*John* 1: 1-3)

John then suggests that the Word was Jesus Christ who was the only begotten Son of God:

And the Word became flesh and dwelt among us, full of grace and truth; we have beheld his glory, glory as the only Son from the Father. (*John* 1: 14)

The word 'flesh' in the above quotation meant that Jesus came to the earth as a real human being revealing the one God, and he was a real human being even following his 'resurrection'. He remained a real human being during the appearances to the disciples until he ascended into heaven where he returned to the right hand of God.

The object of John's Gospel is summarized as follows:

Now Jesus did many other signs in the presence of the disciples, which are not written in this book; but these are written that you may believe that Jesus is the Christ, the Son of God, and that believing you may have life in his name. (*John* 20: 30-31)

In John the disciples may have experienced an illusion of the presence of Jesus on the evening of the first day. When the above account was written, about seventy years following the event, it addressed the wider theological concern of the physical nature of the 'resurrected' Christ. According to the author of the Gospel of John, however, this first encounter involved: 1) the disciples seeing an apparition of Jesus; 2) the apparition eating a piece of broiled fish; and 3) the apparition talking to the disciples. Except for the eating of fish the remaining reported experiences are well within the boundaries of normal grief-related experiences. When the above encounter was reported to Thomas he did not believe the story.

Eight days later, in the presence of Thomas, Jesus appeared again and Jesus asked Thomas to touch him in order to prove that Jesus was real flesh and blood. Thus, the physical reality of the 'resurrected' Jesus was confirmed. Once again the author of John may have woven core grief experiences into a story which was supposed to confirm the physical nature of the resurrected Christ. But as we have seen, Dr Shuchter reported that the illusion of being touched by the deceased or touching an apparition of the deceased is now considered to be a normal grief-related hallucination.

In C. Murray Parkes' article, *Seeking and 'Finding' a Lost Object: Evidence from Recent Studies of the Reaction to Bereavement* (Ellard, p.223), he reports that the bereaved search restlessly to recover the deceased. One widow reported:

'I can picture him in any given circumstances... I can almost feel his skin and touch his hands...' (Ellard, p.223)

We have mentioned that the third appearance of Jesus to the disciples in the Gospel of John was on the beach at the Sea of Tiberias. Norman Perrin argues in his book *The New Testament: An Introduction* that the Gospel of John originally ended at *John* 20: 31. The epilogue, *John* 21: 1-25, which contains the Sea of Tiberias story, was a later addition to the text. Perrin wrote:

Chapter 21 has been added as an epilogue by another writer... The purpose of the epilogue seems to be ecclesiastical. (Perrin, p.361)

Yet the author of the epilogue 'knows a tradition of a resurrection appearance to the disciples in Galilee as they were fishing, and he preserves it as a supplement to the accounts of the appearances in Jerusalem' (Perrin, p.361).

At the Sea of Tiberias the disciples recognized Jesus while they were still in the boat, and when they got out on the land:

> ... they saw a charcoal fire there, with fish lying on it, and bread. Jesus said to them, 'Bring some of the fish that you have just caught.' So Simon Peter went aboard and hauled the net ashore, full of large fish, a hundred and fifty-three of them; and although there were so many, the net was not torn. Jesus said to them, 'Come and have breakfast.' Now none of the disciples dared ask him, 'Who are you?' They knew it was the Lord. Jesus came and took the bread and gave it to them, and so with the fish. This was now the third time that Jesus was revealed to the disciples after he was raised from the dead. (*John* 21: 9-14)

Grief does end in a short period of time and grief-related hallucinations are most common in the first months following the death of someone who was loved. Thus, wherever the disciples went they took their grief with them. We will never know what the central grief-related experience was at the Sea of Tiberias or even if there was one but it is possible that the disciples had the illusion of the appearance of Jesus on the beach or in fact one of the disciples saw an apparition of Jesus. These core experiences were then magnified and enlarged according to the process described above.

The distinguished Anglican Bishop John Shelby Spong recently published his book *Resurrection Myth or Reality*. (Spong, pp.249-255) He gives great credence to the Sea of Tiberias story. In fact Spong is the first author I have read who suggests that the disciples might have experienced grief following the death of Jesus. Yet, he is very timid in suggesting that apparitions might have been involved in the disciples' experiences, and he rejects this idea.

Spong spends many pages telling how the disciples returned to their profession of being fishermen. He also suggests that in the early morning hours, on the shores of the Sea of Tiberias, the disciples might have seen mists in the air which could have been mistaken for apparitions. Spong writes:

> There were times in that early darkness that the mist on the lake looked like apparitions. *Grieving people do tend to see forms that speak to their grief.* Simon once thought he saw a ghost-like figure walking on the sea. It was so real that he actually rose and walked out into the

water to get a better view. When he was waist-deep in the water, the misty apparition seemed to evaporate, so Simon returned to the beach, shaken, and wondering why his mind played tricks on him. (Spong, p.249, my italics)

A very realistic question must be asked: How could Bishop Spong, who was writing in 1994, know that there was a mist on the Sea of Tiberias almost 2000 years ago, and how did Bishop Spong know that Peter walked into the water until it was waist-deep?

Spong now locates the resurrection event in the experiences of Peter (Simon) at the Sea of Tiberias. Spong wrote:

Suddenly it all came together for Simon. The crucifixion was not puni-tive, it was intentional. The cross was Jesus' ultimate parable, acted out on the stage of history to open the eyes of those whose eyes could be opened in no other way to the meaning of Jesus as the sign of God's love... Simon saw the meaning of the crucifixion that morning as he had never before seen it, and Simon felt himself to be embraced even with his doubts, his fears, his denials in a way that he had never before been embraced. *That was the dawn of Easter in human history.* It would be fair to say that in that moment *Simon felt resurrected.* The clouds of his *grief, confusion, and depression* vanished from his mind, and in that moment he knew that Jesus was part of the very essence of God, and *at that moment Simon saw Jesus alive.* (Spong, p.255, my italics)

Spong has the idea that the disciples experienced grief but he does not use the full information that is available from grief studies con-cerning the relationship between hallucinations and grief. It is my contention that the disciples did experience grief and that their lives were changed because of their grief experiences. In fact Spong sug-gests that Simon felt resurrected, but then he makes an error by suggesting that Simon saw Jesus alive. Spong might have emphasized that Simon saw new meaning in Jesus' life, but this does not mean that Jesus was alive.

In Dr Rees' study of widowers and their hallucinations of their dead spouses, it was discovered that those men in the category described as self-employed and engaged in industry and commerce had a 49% chance of experiencing hallucinations following the death of their spouses. Granted, Jesus was not a spouse, but the disciples were very close to him and their chances of experiencing hallucinations were very high.

Underlying the Gospel stories of the 'resurrected' Jesus is a central core of grief-related hallucinations.

The concept of the 'resurrected' Jesus changed from the earliest documents (Paul's) up to the latest (the Gospel of John). Paul, in his letters, wrote that Jesus was 'sown a physical body, [and] raised a spiritual body' (*1 Cor.* 15: 44). Mary Magdalene's encounter with an apparition of Jesus at the tomb was a very clear grief-related hallucination. In the original Gospel of Mark there were no reported appearances to the disciples. In the Gospel of Matthew the disciples' apparitions on the mountain in Galilee were probably very straight-forward grief experiences and there were those who doubted. In the Gospel of Luke the two followers of Jesus saw an apparition of Jesus on the road to Emmaus but now the apparition walked and talked with Jesus' followers. When the two went to Jerusalem Jesus had 'appeared' to the eleven and was supposed to have eaten a piece of fish. Thus, reports of the nature of the apparitions had already changed. Finally, in John the author argues that Jesus was in fact a physically 'resurrected' Christ. Thus, the physically 'resurrected' Christ served the theological purposes of the author of the Gospel of John.

Grief and the Apparitions of Jesus in the Acts of the Apostles (AD85)

In the *Acts of the Apostles* there is yet another account of the events following the crucifixion and 'resurrection' of Jesus. Jesus 'appeared' to the disciples over a forty-day period. (*Acts* 1: 3)

Appearances of the deceased can continue over a period of time following the death of a loved one. There is no common time frame in which appearances can occur, but appearances of the deceased are most frequent 'in the early weeks and months of bereavement. These intrusive images can create overwhelming distress' (Shuchter, p.3). I met a widow in Southern California who saw an appearance of her deceased husband seven years after his death. He suddenly appeared in her living room while she was reading a book and said, 'Sweety, I just returned to let you know that I am alright now.' I asked the widow what this meant to her and she said, 'It meant that I had finally accepted his death.'

The Christian day of the Ascension is on the fortieth day following Easter and marks the close of the post-Resurrection appearances and the elevation of Christ to heaven. (Cross and Livingstone, p.94)

Ten days following the day of the Ascension, on the day of the

Pentecost, 'they were all gathered in one place... And they were all filled with the Holy Spirit and began to speak in other tongues, as the Spirit gave them utterance' (*Acts* 2: 1-4).

Following Peter's speech on this occasion the apostles said to Peter and the rest of the apostles, 'Brethren, what shall we do?' Then 'they devoted themselves to the apostles' teaching and fellowship, to the breaking of bread and prayers' (*Acts* 2: 37, 42).

According to the book of Acts there were key events on the third, fortieth and fiftieth days following the death of Jesus. These events were the Resurrection, the Ascension and the Pentecost, and they seem to parallel what we now know to be another aspect or process of bereavement.

The disciples' pattern of coming to grips with the death of Jesus falls into the normal stages of bereavement as described in contemporary bereavement research. The Acts of the Apostles becomes much more understandable when it is approached from this point of view. It is now possible to understand the biblical accounts as reports of the bereavement experiences of Mary Magdalene and the disciples.

Bereavement is the period of time following a death during which grief occurs, and I want to illustrate this by giving four examples taken from my own ministry.

First, about twelve years ago, I received a telephone call from a friend in Victoria, B.C., advising that her husband had died in the middle of the night from a heart attack. It was traumatic for her to have awakened and discovered that her husband was dead. She notified all appropriate authorities and then she telephoned me and asked if, four days later, I would read his memorial service. I consented.

Following the formal part of the service, the people who had come went to the carport awaiting the casket. Before the casket was carried to the waiting hearse the wife of the deceased requested that the casket be opened which would make it possible for her to place a flower upon the deceased body as a last gesture of farewell. She was sobbing those deep cries which come from the depths of the human spirit.

When the casket was closed the pall-bearers came in and the widow and I walked in front of the casket. We then stepped aside as the casket was placed into the hearse, and then the hearse was driven away. As the hearse left (there was no committal at the grave side) I held the widow in my arms and she said, 'I cannot cry any more. He is gone.'

It seemed to me, at this moment, that she had accepted the fact

41

that her husband was dead and all efforts at continued denial were useless. This act of acceptance was the first major step in her bereavement. Yet, emotional separation was quite a different thing.

In the weeks which followed her husband's memorial service she worked through this traumatic loss. She telephoned me every week and wanted to know what she should do now that her husband was gone. Should she continue to live in Victoria or should she move to Vancouver where she would be with other members of the family? What would her husband want her to do? Should she sell her husband's boat or keep it? Again, what would he want her to do? If she kept the boat, then she would have to learn how to swim and she would have to take the power squadron course.

For several weeks these telephone calls continued and I would simply say that as time passed she would be able to decide what she wanted to do and it would all become very clear to her.

One day she telephoned and her voice was completely changed. She said, 'I know what I am going to do! I am going to keep my husband's boat; I am going to take the power squadron course; I am going to learn to swim; I am going to look for and buy a business.'

Ten days later she telephoned and said, 'I am doing it! I started today! I have signed up for the power squadron course. I have enrolled for swimming lessons. I have started looking for a business. I am on my way!'

I am not suggesting that this widow's bereavement period was over, but the acute stage of bereavement was over. When the number of days were counted for this change to come about, it was exactly 41 days from her husband's death to the telephone call in which she said that she knew what she was going to do, and it was exactly 51 days from his death to the point where she said she was beginning to do what she wanted to do.

This period is significant because it shows three stages in her bereavement process, and although it is only one case, it is very close to the time period for the bereavement process of Mary Magdalene and the disciples, who accepted the death of Jesus in 3 days, in 40 days decided what they wanted to do, and on the 50th day began to do it.

Second, on Friday 31 March 1995 I was telephoned by a friend of mine whose wife was approaching death from a fatal case of leukaemia. He wanted me to meet with his immediate family and sit by the side of his dying wife. I immediately consented and was taken to his home where the family had gathered. When I sat with the dying woman she could not speak and she did not recognize me.

After sitting with her for a period of time I went into their living room where we made preparations for a memorial service which would take place when she actually died. When this meeting was over I returned home to await the news of her death.

At about 8.00 pm on that same day I received a telephone call advising me that she had died and the funeral service would be on Wednesday 5 April 1995 at 11.00 am. The only person who was sitting by her side at the moment of death was her daughter Helen. Helen is about 34 years old.

On Sunday morning at 11.30 am I received a telephone call from Helen advising me that she had gone for a walk in a wooded area which was on their property. She had been walking on the trail for only a few minutes when she looked up and in front of her, about 200 feet away, she saw her mother walking towards her with her head down. Helen stopped walking but her mother continued toward her and when her mother was only about 50 feet away she suddenly disappeared.

Helen called because she was worried that she might be losing her mind and what did I think of what happened to her? I explained the relationship between grief and grief-related appearances. I told her that she would not have had such an experience unless she had a very deep attachment to her mother and she should be grateful for having had such a positive experience. These experiences are usually helpful accompaniments of grief. (Rees, p.37) I encouraged her to think about all of the feelings she had towards her mother and to know that such an illusion is a normal part of grief. She was relieved and it turned out that her grieving pattern was quite severe, involving some physical complications. It is important to know that she sought good medical assistance and she learned a lot about the meaning of grief in her life.

From Helen's bereavement pattern I know that it was absolutely possible that Mary Magdalene could have seen an appearance of Jesus on the first day of the week or Easter morning. Helen's mother died on Friday evening and Helen saw her appearance on Sunday morning. Two thousand years ago no one understood the emotional struggles involved with grief and they would have literally believed that Jesus was 'resurrected'.

The experiences of Mary Magdalene and the disciples now appear to be very normal grief-related illusions. I would not presume to argue

43

that we can know what 'really' happened to them, but the similarities between the grief-related illusions of the followers of Jesus and those now known to accompany normal grief are indeed striking.

Third, about four years ago I spoke to the Unitarian Church in Victoria B.C. about the core grief-related appearances and illusions which can accompany grief. When the morning service was over and after I had talked to a number of people, one woman asked if she might have a word with me. I talked with her and this was her story.

Two years previously her twenty-year-old son had been killed in a horrible automobile accident. He had been visiting friends and as he was driving home at about two in the morning, a young man who was driving a pickup truck ran a red light and collided with her son's car in the middle of the intersection. Both were instantly killed.

Naturally, this was traumatic for her and of course all funeral preparations were made and the normal burial events were completed.

Two weeks following his burial, however, she was awakened at about 2.00am by some very distinct noises in the house. Her husband was away at the time. She heard the front door open and her son said, 'It is OK, Mom. I am home now.' Her son had always made it a point to tell his mother when he came home because he knew that she would never go to sleep until he was safely home. Then she heard her son walk up the stairs, turn on the bedroom lights, make his preparations for going to bed, and then he turned out the light.

This woman was transfixed by hearing her son, so she jumped out of bed and ran up the stairs to his room, only to find it empty.

Then she told me that she had never told anyone about this, because she thought that other people would think that she was crazy and they might want to put her in a hospital. I explained as clearly as I could that in current grief research such auditory illusions are very common in grief. I also explained that in grief very normal people undergo extreme stress and the mind can attempt to recover the deceased in this and other ways. I suggested that she explore the meaning of her son's death through loss counselling, because it would be very important to make sure that she understood the emotional impact of such an enormous loss on her mental health.

Auditory illusions are in the grief experiences of Mary Magdalene. It is very clear that Jesus spoke to her, and because of the utter reality of the situation, as perceived by Mary, she spoke to Jesus. Thus, auditory illusions can be a very normal part of grief. Such conversations, however, cannot be used as evidence for resurrection.

44

They constitute evidence for grief.

Fourth, the following grief-related illusion is very complicated because the person who had the experience holds the point of view that what happened to her was not an illusion because it was so very real. It is necessary, therefore, to restate my preliminary value judgments with regard to resurrection.

I hold to the point of view that when a human being is dead then that human being is dead. There never was nor will there ever be a resurrection of a body if that body was in fact dead. Yet, we also know that people can develop very deep psychological attachments to one another, and when a person who has very deep attachments to others dies, those who are living must cope with the emotional attachments which are still very much alive. Dealing with these emotional attachments is bereavement or grief.

This story involves a woman whose name is Nancy[5] and she is a very highly trained social worker who has specialized in psychological counselling. She holds an excellent job with the Province of British Columbia in their Department of Human Resources and in her field she is quite sophisticated.

Here is the story.

Nancy had known a lovely young man, Bill[6], who had the capacity of relating to people at very significant levels of their personality. Nancy and I both attended his memorial service where I was asked to read two readings which were relevant to his life. This memorial service was held outdoors on the banks of the Puntledge river in Courtenay B.C. There were about two hundred and fifty people who came to pay their last respects to Bill.

About a year after his memorial service I met Nancy and we had coffee, at which time she told me about the encounter she had with Bill following his death. She was hiking in a very beautiful park, Strathcona Park, which is on Vancouver Island. She was hiking with a girl friend when 'suddenly completely out of the blue, I was aware of the presence of Bill... I have no recollection of thinking or talking about him before this experience. There were no visual, auditory or sensory clues. Simply a crystal clear sense that Bill was with me. It was so clear that I shouted to my hiking companion to "Be quiet... Bill's here."

'I was completely silent, and for the next approximately twenty minutes I "walked with Bill." There was no conversation, only a profound sense of him – including his humour, playfulness and love.

45

There was also a great sense of comfort. I was less clear when he left me – but after a few minutes of not sensing him – I started to talk to my companion again.'

This brief encounter had a profound impact upon Nancy. When Nancy had known Bill in previous years they often went walking together. Bill always wanted to walk in the woods or in the mountains, but Nancy was afraid to walk in those areas. She was afraid that wild animals might kill her or that she might get lost, so her phobia against walking in the woods was important. The result was that Bill and Nancy would walk on the beach or at the seashore.

Nancy had tried several times to rid herself of this phobia. She even went to a summer outdoor school in the mountains but the phobia never left her. Yet, after this brief encounter with Bill her phobia disappeared and her fear of walking in the mountains was gone. Nancy wrote: 'But after that walk in the mountains, my fear largely dissipated. It was not that I sensed Bill protecting me but rather that I was given the love of the mountains/woods which surpassed the fear. It was a wonderful gift from Bill.'

Nancy wrote that she 'was aware of the presence of Bill.' Of course to Nancy his presence was real and the resolution of her phobia about walking in the mountains/woods simply confirmed the presence of Bill.[7] I believe we are forced to take this experience at face value, but we must be reminded that in the studies done by Dr Shuchter this very kind of experience is the most common one in spousal bereavement. Dr Shuchter would not detract from the *meaning* of this experience but he would also be aware that the unconscious can work in such a way that it seemed to Nancy as though what happened came from Bill. The very nature of an illusion is its utter realness. Whatever else it might have been, it was a psychological gift which was of great meaning to Nancy.

When we look back at the stories which became the founding events in the Christian Church we are reminded of two events which were similar to the experience of Nancy. There is the road to Emmaus story, and the disciples' encounter with Jesus on the mountain in Galilee.

To summarize my argument thus far, one way of looking at the biblical accounts of the Resurrection, the Ascension, and the Pentecost is to assume that the records might have a possible relationship to bereavement.

1. Mary Magdalene, the disciples, and the wider public were at-

tracted to Jesus of Nazareth because of his charisma. Thus, he became a prophet to his followers.

2. Jesus was perceived by the ruling party of Sadducees and the Romans as being a threat to their ruling powers. The Pharisees as exemplified by Gamaliel did not object to the teachings of Jesus and his followers.

3. Jesus was tried, sentenced, and crucified by the Romans and was presumably buried in a tomb. However, even if he was never buried in a tomb this would have had no bearing on the subsequent grief of Mary Magdalene and the disciples.

4. Following the death of Jesus his followers were plunged into profound grief and as a consequence they may have experienced grief-related hallucinations of Jesus. Today, we know that such hallucinations are normal grief experiences, where both the conscious and unconscious minds of the grieving person search desperately to maintain ties with the deceased.

5. Those who are grieving can experience five different types of hallucinations following the death of a loved one. Mary Magdalene and the disciples probably experienced all five types of hallucinations immediately following the death of Jesus of Nazareth. On the basis of these hallucinations they believed that Jesus of Nazareth had actually been physically 'resurrected' from the dead.

6. Following the Easter events the disciples continued to experience hallucinations of Jesus for forty days. During this forty-day period the disciples experienced normal bereavement. They had to come to grips with the sudden death of Jesus. They were plunged into grief and experienced uncertainty, fear, guilt, anxiety, and denial. Gradually, they re-evaluated their lives by working through their loss. They are reported to have been at different places in Galilee, Jerusalem, and Bethany. Wherever they went, however, they took their grief with them.

7. After forty days they regained their confidence; and, when their confidence returned, they were no longer emotionally dependent on Jesus of Nazareth. Thus, I believe the 'Ascension' was the externalization of their inward renewal. That is, they had freed themselves from their emotional dependence upon the prophet and had recovered some of their projections from Jesus.

8. On the fiftieth day, the day of the Pentecost, the disciples accepted a new role for themselves and this is signalled by their asking Peter and the apostles the question, 'Brethren, what shall we do?'

47

9. Thus, the acute bereavement period was over and the central Christian myth had been constructed. Mary Magdalene and the disciples were participants in the development of the myth of the Resurrection, the Ascension, and the Pentecost.

10. According to the Gospel writers the central message of the disciples changed from the teachings of the historical Jesus to their belief that Jesus of Nazareth had been actually resurrected from the dead. The disciples were now changed into apostles and they went forth to preach the good news.

11. I argue further that the grief experiences of Mary Magdalene and the disciples were very similar to the grief experiences which people have today. It is also true that the grief experiences reported in the New Testament were probably exaggerated to serve the purposes of the authors of the Gospels.

Chapter 4

Conversion Disorder and Paul's Belief in the Resurrected Jesus Christ

Thus far I have discussed resurrection as it relates to the Gospel stories. In those stories we traced the experiences of Mary Magdalene and the disciples, and then suggested that they experienced grief-related hallucinations following the death of Jesus. It was these very normal appearances and other illusions which led them to believe that they had actually seen the 'resurrected' Jesus.

Now I must turn my attention to the apostle Paul, because he thought that God had resurrected Jesus from the dead and presented Jesus to him in his psychological trauma on the road to Damascus, which occurred somewhere between six to eleven years following the death of Jesus. In Christian theology this is referred to as the CHRIST EVENT. I want to look at this event, not from a theological point of view, but from the point of view of psychology. If it turns out that this experience does not constitute evidence for Jesus' 'resurrection', it can still be seen as another source for the emergence of the myth of the resurrected Jesus Christ, developed mainly by Paul.

I believe that Paul experienced what is called in psychiatry an episode of conversion disorder, and that Jesus of Nazareth was never resurrected from the dead as believed by Paul. It will be further argued that Paul's religious outlook makes perfect sense when it is looked at from the perspective of conversion disorder. Attempts by many theologians to explain Paul's experience as a 'religious conversion' (in this instance meaning the changing from one religion to another), or a 'call', have been lacking in many respects because they fail to account for the physical and emotional aspects of what happened to Paul. My hypothesis that Paul experienced conversion disorder will account for the symptoms recorded in the book of Acts and in his own letters, and it will shed new light on the meaning of the religion which evolved from Paul's experience.

It is important to clarify what occurs in conversion disorder and then review the evidence contained in the New Testament with regard to Paul.

In *The Diagnostic and Statistical Manual of Mental Disorders*, third edition (DSM III), published by the American Psychiatric Association, conversion disorder is defined as follows: 'The essential feature is a clinical picture in which the predominant disturbance is a loss of or alteration in physical functioning that suggests physical disorder *but which instead is apparently an expression of a psychological conflict or need.* The disturbance is not under voluntary control, and after appropriate investigation cannot be explained by any physical disorder or known pathological mechanism' (my italics, Spitzer, p.244). It must be made very clear that conversion disorder is a psychiatric term and not a religious term. It does not refer to a person's being converted from one religion to another. If a person has a serious emotional conflict over religious matters, then conversion disorder may be a consequence but *the disorder occurs when the unconscious disables a person physically and sometimes psychologically in order to resolve an unresolved emotional conflict.*

In my ministry of forty-eight years I have been involved with only one episode of conversion disorder. This occurred in 1967 while I was the minister of the First Unitarian Church of Chicago. One day a member of our church telephoned and told me that her son, Billy, was in hospital and he was experiencing paralysis of his hands. The doctors had given him all relevant medical tests but had found nothing wrong. She asked me if I would visit him. Of course I did.

Before I went to see him, however, I called his doctor who told me that he had turned the case over to a psychiatrist, and before I went to visit the young man I had better have a meeting with the new doctor. I called the psychiatrist, and he said that the young man was experiencing an episode of conversion disorder.

This is what brought on the episode. In this family there were four boys and all of them were musicians. The mother was a concert pianist, and Billy was the last child. At an early age he became interested in playing the lute, and the family arranged for him to have lessons. By the age of thirteen he was an accomplished lute player. However, he had never played for anyone other than his teacher and the members of his family.

Billy continued to practise and play for the family but he flatly refused to play for the general public. His mother knew that Billy had a problem playing before strangers, so one day, around his eighteenth birthday, she asked him if he would play for her music club. He was delighted and began to get his programme in order, and all went well until the morning before. About 1.00am on the day of the concert his hands began to experience tingling, and by early morning they were paralysed. He was rushed to the hospital where he was given tests and there were no physical reasons why he should be experiencing paralysis. Of course he never gave the concert.

Within a few days the psychiatrist had uncovered the fact that Billy was afraid to play in public because he might miss one note and embarrass himself and, in this case, both himself and his mother. Thus, through paralysis, the unconscious prevented him from playing, even though he, logically, wanted to do it. Within a few weeks he was back to normal and he then understood why he was afraid to play.

Billy's episode of conversion disorder was very simple, with no complicated emotional overtones; but some episodes of conversion disorder can be very complicated and they can involve many symptoms and cause considerable distress. The following example is taken from the writings of Dr Michael Kenny and it is a good example.

Dr Michael Kenny, who is a professor of anthropology at Simon Fraser University, wrote the book *The Passion of Ansel Bourne*. This is the story of a man who suffered an episode of conversion disorder on 28 October 1857 on a road near Westerly, Rhode Island. This episode carries with it physical disorder as well as psychological and religious overtones.

On 17 November 1857 the *Providence Daily Journal* reported that Bourne's experience might be looked upon as a miracle 'that may be placed by the side of the conversion of S Paul.' Dr Kenny described Bourne's experience as follows:

> On October 28, 1857, Bourne – a carpenter – left his home and set off for the nearby town of Westerly, Rhode Island, but he did not arrive. As he walked quickly along, he was conscious of no unusual feelings, until a thought came up vividly in his mind that he ought to go to a meeting (a local church meeting). This thought was connected with no conscientious feeling of duty to go to a meeting, but seemed a mere internal and unaccountable suggestion. To the suggestion he answered, '*Where?*' To this inquiry he was answered in the same manner, '*To the Christian Chapel.*' *His spirit rose up against this idea*

*in decided and bitter opposition, and he said within himself, 'I would
rather be struck deaf and dumb forever, than go there.'*

Shortly, Bourne felt dizzy and sat down on a rock beside the way-
side; a wagon approached and as he watched, *'it seemed as though
some powerful hand drew something down over his head, and then
over his face, and finally over his whole body, depriving him of his
sight, his hearing, and his speech, and rendering him perfectly help-
less.'* Bourne was taken home in the wagon and his doctor hastily
summoned; tests were performed but no response could be evoked,
and the doctor reported that 'he was in fact perfectly insensible.'
However, Bourne himself would claim that, though his major senses
were gone, he was fully conscious of having been taken to bed and of
the ministrations of doctor and family. In this personal darkness his
thoughts went back over the preceding events and *he concluded that
he had been touched by the hand of God.*

While in blackness Bourne reviewed the condition of his soul and
found it sadly wanting: *he was estranged from his fellow men and from
a God* whom he had denied. 'This silence was as though the soul had
been cast into a deep, bottomless and shoreless sepulchre, where dismal
silence was to reign eternally. And it was also night there without a
single ray of light.' As one justly cast off from God, he felt the horrors
of that dreadful idea – cast into outer darkness. He fully acknowledged
the justice of God in his condemnation, and spurned from his soul the
thought of insulting God by asking mercy for such a sinner. *The only
offering he could think to make of himself was as a victim of sins too
great for even the mercy of God*, and as an offering fit only for the
fiery sword of justice. A day later, after many thoughts such as these,
his sight was suddenly restored, but still he was isolated *by lack of
speech and hearing.* In order to communicate, he requested writing
materials and, while his wife was out of the room to fetch them, a new
thought came unbidden into Bourne's mind: *'Are you now willing to
ask for forgiveness of all whom you have injured?'* He assented, and
those whom he believed himself to have harmed were summoned to
his bedside where, while silently weeping, *he asked their forgiveness*
through the medium of a slate and piece of chalk.

Bourne was taken several times to the Christian Chapel, and there,
through the minister who read what he wrote on the slate, made public
amends before God and man. On Sunday, November 15, Bourne wrote:
'I have been led to think, while sitting here, *why I have been called
from the ranks of sinners, and I have been led to think that God has
something for me to do.* Why I have come up here to the place of all
others which three weeks ago I would have shunned, I know not... Why
I feel as I do this afternoon, I cannot tell, but I do feel as though God

was about to speak to Westerly, in what way I do not know – but oh, *may God's will be done!' What then occurred was widely regarded as a miracle. Bourne's hearing and speech were instantly restored.* He cried: 'Glory to God and the Lamb forever!' and fell on his knees to pray before the amazed congregation. As he went home from this extraordinary scene, 'he could hear... the voice of the Lord in each rustling leaf.'

His health steadily improved, and he rejoiced in glorifying God until, on Saturday, November 28, Bourne suffered another attack and was certain he would die on that night. But he awoke Sunday morning with the words in his mouth, 'I yet live!' and then, in the small hours of Sunday night, *he had a vision.* As Bourne lay in bed, *suddenly his room seemed all lighted up with the most extraordinary brightness, brighter than the light of day.* He started with surprise, and saw an image or appearance, like a man in form, standing by the side of his bed. There appeared nothing like a face, but in place of it *there was an appearance like the sun shining in his brightness. A voice, which seemed to proceed from the image* before him, said: *'Settle up your earthly business, and go to work for me.'* Bourne woke his wife and asked if she had seen anything, but she had not. Then as Bourne held his wife's hand, the vision returned, and once more he was unable to speak or move. It said: 'Settle up your worldly business, and go to work for me. Your family shall be taken care of, and yourself looked out for. Go, open your mouth and I will fill it. Go, tell the world what your eyes have seen, and your ears have heard.'

Ansel Bourne obeyed this command, and as his friends reported: 'Mr. Bourne has left his worldly occupation – a carpenter – to work for Him who was once known on earth as 'The Carpenter's Son' (my italics, Kenny, pp.64-66).

Kenny suggested that Bourne had experienced conversion disorder. Bourne's conversion disorder involved loss of sight, hearing, speech, and motor coordination. He saw lights and had a vision. His emotional conflicts revolved around his feelings of guilt in relationship to his family and to his friends. In some deep way he felt as though he was a guilty sinner and proceeded to ask for forgiveness from all whom he thought he had injured. Out of this experience he changed his occupation from being a carpenter to being an itinerant preacher. Ansel Bourne is an example of just how complicated conversion disorder can be.

I will turn once again to the American Psychiatric Association's book *The Diagnostic and Statistical Manual of Mental Disorders,* third edition or DSM III. In this work the following medical analysis of conversion disorder is presented.

The most obvious psychiatric conversion disorder symptoms are those that resemble neurological disease, such as loss of motor co-ordination, paralysis and blindness.

Psychiatrists have suggested that there are two mechanisms which explain what the individual derives from having a conversion symptom. In one mechanism, the individual achieves a primary gain by keeping an 'internal conflict or need out of awareness'. In these cases there is a direct relationship between an environmental stimulus and an inner conflict. In the other mechanism, the individual achieves secondary gain 'by avoiding a particular activity that is noxious to him or her.'

There are several features of conversion reaction or disorder which are of great interest to us in this discussion. The symptoms usually develop 'in a setting of extreme psychological stress', and they appear suddenly and without prior warning. Conversion disorder is usually of short duration 'with abrupt onset and resolution'. The impact on the individual's life is usually marked and can prevent normal life activities.

Turning our attention back to Paul, there is one predisposing factor which is especially relevant to his converson disorder. It is witnessing 'the recent death of a significant figure' in one's life. (Spitzer, pp.244-245) Paul had just organized and witnessed the agonizing murder of Stephen. The internal stress of having participated in the murder of Stephen might have caused sufficient internal conflict to have precipitated his conversion disorder. Yet his teacher, Gamaliel, warned that the followers of Jesus should not be persecuted. This too contributed to his emotional conflict. I will discuss this in greater detail in the next chapter.

DSM III then presents the diagnostic criteria for conversion disorder. I will list the diagnostic criteria and concurrently analyse what happened to Paul, in order to show that his experiences might constitute sufficient evidence for conversion disorder. (The diagnostic criteria are in capital letters).

THE PREDOMINANT DISTURBANCE IS A LOSS OF, OR ALTERATION IN PHYSICAL FUNCTIONING, SUGGESTING PHYSICAL DISORDER.
As Paul was walking on the road to Damascus he fell to the ground. *This means that he suddenly lost the motor coordination in his legs.* When he opened his eyes he was blind.

54

PSYCHOLOGICAL FACTORS ARE JUDGED TO BE THE CAUSE OF THE SYMPTOM, AS EVIDENCED BY ONE OF THE FOLLOWING:

(1) THERE IS A TEMPORAL RELATIONSHIP BETWEEN AN ENVIRONMENTAL STIMULUS THAT IS APPARENTLY RELATED TO A PSYCHOLOGICAL CONFLICT, OR NEED, AND THE INITIATION OR EXACERBATION OF THE SYMPTOM.

Paul had been a student under the liberal Rabbi Gamaliel. Gamaliel had argued before the Sanhedrin that the followers of Jesus should not be persecuted. In this matter Gamaliel spoke with great strength and determination because he was the accepted leader of the popular Pharisees. Paul would have been familiar with the arguments against persecuting the followers of THE WAY.

Yet, whatever the reasons might have been, Paul associated himself with the High Priest, who was the leader of the Sadducees, and he believed that the followers of Jesus should be put in chains and consigned to prison or, in some instances, murdered.

It is highly probable that Paul, against the wishes of his teacher Gamaliel, organized the stoning to death of Stephen. The evidence for this rests on the simple fact that those who murdered Stephen laid their coats at the feet of Paul. This experience must have weighed heavily on Paul, and would have been a predisposing factor for conversion disorder, since the murder of Stephen had occurred only a short time before Paul obtained permission to go to Damascus.

In addition to the stoning to death of Stephen, Paul had continued to wreak havoc on the followers of THE WAY. He would go to their homes, drag them out into the street, and take them to prison.

Paul went to the High Priest and obtained a letter authorizing him to go to Damascus where he would carry out his continued persecution of the followers of Jesus.

The High Priest approved of Paul's persecutions. However Paul's teacher and previous mentor, Gamaliel, had argued that the followers of Jesus should not be persecuted. This was the fundamental emotional conflict which was in Paul's unconscious.

When Paul reached the outskirts of Damascus he realized that he would soon be persecuting the followers of THE WAY once again. The conflict between his conscious intent to continue the persecution and the unconscious injunction from his rabbi not to persecute the followers of THE WAY, led to his conversion disorder. The closer Paul got to Damascus the more intense the unresolved conflict became.

Finally, conversion disorder set in. He experienced temporary motor difficulties by falling to the ground and he was blinded. His blindness would have prevented him from carrying out the wishes of the High Priest.

THE SYMPTOM ENABLES THE INDIVIDUAL TO AVOID SOME ACTIVITY THAT IS NOXIOUS TO HIM OR HER.

As a result of his blindness he would have been prevented from carrying out his mission which was to put the followers of THE WAY in chains and take them back to Jerusalem.

IT HAS BEEN DETERMINED THAT THE SYMPTOM IS NOT UNDER VOLUNTARY CONTROL.

This is consistent with what happened to Paul. He was walking along the road and suddenly fell to the ground and was blinded. This was not under voluntary control. This characteristic of conversion disorder is very important because it led Paul to believe that what happened to him was an act of God. Also Paul would never have known what really happened to him. In Paul's own description of this event he did not know whether what happened to him was in his body or out of his body. He repeatedly said that only God knows what happened. This is consistent with the involuntary nature of conversion disorder.

There is one remaining symptom exhibited by Paul during his episode of conversion disorder which is of great importance. This was hearing what he thought was the voice of Jesus. I believe that the concept of Jesus Christ flows out of this auditory experience. The Acts of the Apostles reports three times that when Paul fell to the ground he heard a voice which said to him, 'Paul, Paul[8] why do you persecute me?' And Paul asked, 'Who are you, Lord?' And the voice said, 'I am Jesus, whom you are persecuting; but rise, enter the city, and you will be told what you are to do.'

The critical question is this: Where did the voice come from? This is critical because the only constant in the description of Paul's experience in Acts is the hearing of the voice, and this event took place between AD 36 and 41. In Paul's own description of this event he was not at all clear as to what happened to him. Paul used three different Greek words to describe his experience. Jesus appeared; Jesus was seen; Jesus was revealed. It must be noted that the English translation of the Greek could have been translated in other ways.

Furthermore, as we have seen, in the description of his experience Paul wrote that he did not know whether his experience was in the body or out of the body – only God knew.

I think the answer is to be found in the symptoms which can accompany conversion disorder. It is important to know that conversion disorder can be quite simple, as in the case of Billy, and extremely complicated, as in the case of Ansel Bourne and of Paul. In W. Mayer-Gross' book *Clinical Psychiatry* he indicates that in conversion disorder (he uses the word hysteria which is clarified in the next paragraph), emotional experiences of a highly complex kind can occur. These experiences could be of a 'religious kind, including massive and complicated *visual and auditory hallucinations*, internally coherent, and the receipt of "messages" supposedly from God or His angels.' These messages bear the stamp of the personality of the recipient and 'may contain elements of genuine and exalted mysticism' (my italics, Mayer-Gross, p.134). I argue that this is what Paul experienced and the *seeing of lights and the hearing of voices* can accompany conversion disorder.

Since what we are considering at this point can be quite confusing, and before we consider the work of William James, it is necessary to clarify the terminology of conversion disorder. This is necessary because the terminology has changed since the turn of this century. The problem which we are considering, now called 'conversion disorder', is caused by unresolved emotional conflicts coming to resolution in a process in which the unconscious disables the subject in physical or mental ways, or perhaps both. William James, writing without the knowledge of psychological work to come, realized that religious conversion at least involved serious emotional disturbances. Freud, writing first about hysteria, characterized conversion as hysteria or conversion hysteria. Later psychological work led to the emotional and physical phenomenon being called 'conversion disorder'. This is the term used in DSM III. Thus, 'religious conversion' to James was just a singular phenomenon; however, to Freud it was hysteria or conversion hysteria with religious connotations. To modern psychiatry religious conversion is just a religious form of the general problem 'conversion disorder' (Archer).[9] I will sometimes refer to 'religious conversion' as 'conversion disorder with religious overtones'. Now we will turn to William James.

In 1901 William James, the well-known American psychologist, delivered the Gifford Lectures in Edinburgh. These lectures were later published in the book *The Varieties of Religious Experience*. Two chapters of the book are devoted to the study of religious conversion. The cases described by James are instances of *conversion disorder with religious overtones*. The symptoms which accompany religious conversion (James' term) are quite varied and in many respects identical to the religious dimension which can accompany conversion disorder. *However, I argue that Paul did not experience a change from one religion to another – that is from Judaism to Christianity.* The difficulty which most scholars have had in understanding what happened to Paul is at this precise point. Conversion disorder can contain the feelings of unification with a higher power, which can be a religious component of the experience, and in the case of Paul he felt that he had been united with the resurrected Jesus Christ. Thus Paul developed *a new religion* which, later, became Christianity. From a strictly theological[10] point of view, however, Paul remained Jewish to the end of his life.

William James suggests that sudden religious conversion or conversion disorder with religious overtones can be a memorable experience. The person who undergoes the religious conversion experience 'seems to himself (or herself) a passive spectator or undergoer of an astounding process performed upon him from above.' The person who undergoes this experience carries away the feeling of its being a miracle rather than a natural process. *Voices are often heard, lights seen, or visions witnessed; automatic motor phenomena occur; and it always seems, after the surrender of the personal will, as if an extraneous higher power had flooded in and taken possession. Moreover the sense of renovation, safety, cleanness, rightness, can be so marvellous and jubilant as well to warrant one's belief in a radically new substantial nature'* (my italics, James, pp.183-85). James had studied hundreds of cases of conversion disorder with religious overtones and the symptoms were varied but several were similar to those experienced by Paul.

Paul's conversion disorder did have religious overtones, which led him to believe that he had been united with a higher power, and in this case it was with the 'resurrected' Jesus Christ. Paul believed that Jesus spoke to him, and from Paul's point of view this could happen only if Jesus had been actually resurrected by God. Paul's conversion disorder arose out of the conflict between his persecution of the followers of Jesus, his recent witnessing and organizing the murder of Stephen and his rabbi's stern injunction that the followers of Jesus should not be persecuted.

The conversion disorder experienced by Paul contained visual and auditory hallucinations, the receipt of messages he attributed to Jesus

Christ, and above all, a sense of unification with Christ which seemed 'as if an extraneous higher power had flooded in and taken possession' (James, p.183) of his being. Since such experiences can be normal in conversion disorder then what happened to the apostle Paul becomes a bit more understandable.

Paul was on the way to Damascus to put the followers of THE WAY (the followers of Jesus) in chains and return them to Jerusalem. The members of the group in Damascus knew that Paul was coming to take them back to Jerusalem. When the group discovered that Paul was blind and staying in the house of Judas, they must have discussed their impending danger, and they designated Ananias to go to Paul and plead with him to not persecute them. Ananias must have said something which led Paul to resolve his unconscious conflict. He might have said something like this:[11] 'Paul, we know why you have come to Damascus. You have come to take us back to Jerusalem. We also know that you have the authority of the Chief Priest in order to carry out this assignment, but Paul, we plead with you to leave us alone. We remind you that your teacher Gamaliel has argued that we should not be persecuted. Paul, DO NOT PERSECUTE US!'

Ananias' plea to Paul, whatever it was, resolved Paul's unconscious conflict in favour of his rabbi and against the High Priest. When this occurred his sight returned and he was baptized into the Damascus group. However, Paul began to develop a religion which was quite different from the followers of THE WAY, and Paul's religion was based on his experience of unification with what he believed was the resurrected Jesus Christ. Instead of recognizing Ananias as the source of his conflict resolution, Paul attributed his personal forgiveness to the 'resurrected' Jesus Christ.

It is very difficult for us to imagine what a powerful impact this conversion disorder experience must have had on Paul's approach to religion and life. He was absolutely convinced that Jesus had spoken to him on the road to Damascus. This confirmed the 'resurrection' of Jesus by God, and if Jesus was resurrected by God then Jesus must be the Messiah or Christ. It is clear that Paul's new religion, arising out of the religious dimension of his conversion disorder, would be remarkably different from that of Jesus and his brother James. Paul and James would never be able to reconcile their differences.

Paul's traumatic experience contained two dimensions, and they were both physical and mystical. First, the conversion disorder made Paul lose the motor coordination in his legs; it caused complicated visual and auditory hallucinations, and it made him believe that he had received messages from Jesus Christ. Second, this same experience also contained elements of genuine mysticism. In the words of William James, Paul felt as though he had undergone 'an astounding process performed upon him from above'. Thus, new levels of consciousness were opened up within Paul's being. Paul came to believe that Christ was immortal, and if Christ was immortal then Christ could reveal himself and his desires to Paul. These messages came to Paul as a special level of consciousness within himself and they were all internally consistent. Paul wrote concerning the exceeding greatness of the revelations, especially when he was

> 'caught up even to the third Heaven... into paradise, and heard unspeakable words, which it is not lawful for a man to utter' (*2 Cor.* 12: 1-7).

In this quotation it is important to see the different levels of consciousness operating in Paul.

Rolland Emerson Wolfe suggested that Paul believed '... that he had direct communication with Heaven. He insisted that he could present questions and receive directives in answer. His most important dealings were claimed to have been with the immortal Christ' (Wolfe, p.351).

For instance, Paul said his formula for administering the communion of bread and wine had been given him directly by Christ:

> For I received of the Lord that which I delivered unto you... (*1 Cor.* 11: 23)

Paul was certain that most of his teaching had been received by direct commandment from Christ. This claim is expressed where he advised all to

> ... take knowledge of the things which I write to you, that they are the commandment of the Lord. (*1 Cor.* 14: 37)

Again Paul wrote:

> For I make known to you, brethren, as touching the gospel which was preached by me, that it is not after man. For neither did I receive it from man, nor was I taught it, but it came to me through the revelation of Jesus Christ. (*Gal.* 1: 11-12)

Occasionally Paul mentioned having 'no word' from Christ, as:

> I have no commandment from the Lord, but I give my judgment as one who has obtained mercy of the Lord to be trustworthy. (*1 Cor.* 7: 25)

The never-failing love bestowed upon the believer by this mystical Christ is best described in Paul's letter to the Romans.

> Who shall separate us from the love of Christ? Shall tribulation, or anguish, or persecution, or famine, or nakedness, or peril, or sword? ...In all these things we are more than conquerors through him who loved us. For I am persuaded that neither death, nor life, nor angels, nor principalities, nor things present, nor things to come, nor powers, nor height, nor depth, nor any other creation shall be able to separate us from the love of God which is in Christ Jesus our Lord. (*Rom* 8: 35-39)

After Paul's many utterances on the work of Christ, the love of Christ, and the Gospel of Christ, the final word on the mystical indwelling Christ is found in *Colossians* 3: 11-16:

> There cannot be Greek or Jew, circumcised or uncircumcised, barbarian, Scythian, bondsman, freeman: but Christ is all, and in all... and let the peace of Christ rule in your hearts... Let the word of Christ dwell in you richly.

Paul suffered an episode of conversion disorder on the road to Damascus. In that deep trauma he heard a voice which he believed was the voice of the 'resurrected' Jesus of Nazareth. He reasoned that if Jesus 'appeared' and 'spoke' to him then Jesus must still be alive, therefore 'resurrected', therefore the Christ. This inner experience became the psychological foundation for the myth of the resurrected Jesus Christ and the basis for the Christ of Faith.

Chapter 5

The Life and Theology
of the Apostle Paul

As a result of Paul's conversion disorder experience he became the central figure in Christian history, because he founded churches based on his idea of belief in the resurrected Jesus Christ. Without Paul, Jesus and his followers would have been a minor reform movement in Judaism. Hyam Maccoby in his book *The Mythmaker* wrote that Jesus did not found a new religion at all. It was Paul who founded Christianity. Paul used Jesus in the same way that Shakespeare used Hamlet and thereby breathed new imaginative life into Jesus' bones. The Jesus of Paul's story was a fictional character and had no relationship to the Jesus who lived in Nazareth. (Maccoby, p.184)

In order to understand the origins of Christianity it is necessary to know where Paul came from and how he developed his religious ideas. This brief account of his life and thought will give the necessary background to know what actually happened to Paul.

Paul was born in the city of Tarsus, then a thriving seaport on the southern coast of what is now Turkey. Tarsus was a vigorous educational centre, under Greek influence, so Paul would have been thoroughly familiar with Greek thought.

Paul's family was wealthy and Jewish; hence, he would have been raised with an understanding of Hebrew and he would have been introduced to Jewish scriptures, literature and thought. He would have been fluent in both Greek and Hebrew. When he was asked about his background he replied, 'I am a Jew, from Tarsus in Cilicia, a citizen of no mean city' (*Acts* 21: 39).

In the Acts of the Apostles (16: 37, 22: 25-29, 25: 10-12) Paul is presented as having been a Roman citizen from birth. This would imply that his family were Roman citizens; however, it is not known how this citizenship was acquired.

Paul was a bright young man, and at the appropriate age his family sent him to Jerusalem where he became a student under the famous and liberal Rabbi Gamaliel, where he learned the 'law of the fathers.' He also said that he was 'zealous toward God' (*Acts* 22: 3).

Gamaliel was a Pharisee and one of the greatest teachers of Hebraic law in the history of Judaism. He was the first to whom the name RABBAN was given, which identified him as a master teacher. He demonstrated his liberality of thought by making some revisions to the Torah which upgraded the status of women. The Torah is the first five books of Jewish Scripture (Old Testament), and they contain the laws and regulations which were attributed to Moses. The Torah or the law of Moses, or Mosaic law, contains the ten commandments as well as all other regulations which governed the life of the Jewish community.

Gamaliel was a disciple of his grandfather, the famous Rabbi Hillel, who clearly summarized Judaism as follows:

> What is hateful to thee, do not do unto thy fellowman; this is the whole law; the rest is commentary. (Ferm, p.336)

Gamaliel, as the leader of the Pharisees and a member of the Sanhedrin or the ruling council of Israel, favoured leniency at the trial of the disciples when the High Priest brought them before the council. When the disciples told the ruling council what they were teaching the council was enraged

> ... and wanted to kill them. But a Pharisee in the council named Gamaliel, a teacher of the law, held in honour by all the people, stood up and ordered that the men be put outside for a while. And he said to them, 'Men of Israel, take care what you do with these men. For before these days Theudas arose, giving himself out to be somebody, and a number of men, about four hundred, joined him; but he was slain and all who followed him were dispersed and came to nothing. After him Judas the Galilean arose in the days of the census and drew away some of the people after him; he also perished and all who followed him were scattered. So in the present case I tell you, keep away from these men and let them alone; for if this plan or this undertaking is of men, it will fail; but if it is of God, you will not be able to overthrow them. You might even be found opposing God' (*Acts* 5: 33-39).

The above speech by Gamaliel is of great significance because it shows how the Sanhedrin was divided along political lines.

The High Priest was a member of the Sadducees – the party that stood for the interests of the rich and the priestly aristocracy. The Sadducees were never popular in Israel, but they were the ruling party because they cooperated with the hated Roman authorities who actually occupied Israel.

The Sadducees rejected the basic idea of the Pharisees that the law of Moses was open to interpretation from one generation to the next. The Sadducees only accepted the written law. In other religious matters, the Sadducees rejected the ideas of an afterlife, the resurrection of the body, and the existence of angels and spirits. (Cross and Livingstone, p.1222)

The Sadducees were opposed to the teachings of the followers of Jesus and 'they repeatedly attacked the Apostles for teaching the resurrection of Christ' (Cross and Livingstone, p.1222).

The Pharisees, as represented by Gamaliel, saw nothing wrong in the teachings of the followers of Jesus. In fact Gamaliel argued that it would be wrong to persecute them. The Pharisees were held in high regard by the people of Israel and they were valued as a group which accepted religious values in the face of tyranny, supported leniency and mercy in the application of Mosaic law, and championed the rights of the poor against the oppression of the rich. (Maccoby, p.6)

If Paul was indeed a Pharisee who had studied under Gamaliel in his early life he, for some reason, abandoned the Pharisees and became attached to the Sadducees through his association with the High Priest. Paul became a persecutor of the followers of Jesus. This was against the wishes of his teacher Gamaliel, but Paul received continuing support from the High Priest.

When Stephen, one of the disciples, appeared before the council, the members were enraged and 'ground their teeth against him... Then they cast him out of the city and stoned him; and the witnesses laid down their garments at the feet of a young man named Paul' (*Acts* 7: 58-59). 'And Paul was consenting unto his death' (*Acts* 8: 1).

Stephen was stoned to death in front of Paul who organized the whole event with the approval of the High Priest. William Neil in his book *Harper's Bible Commentary* wrote that no doubt Paul was the 'instigator of the stoning of Stephen' (Neil, p.428).

It is possible, as a distant observer, to speculate about Paul's situation at this moment in his life. On the one hand, he had been a Pharisee and, as exemplified by Gamaliel, the Pharisees were not opposed to the teachings of the disciples of Jesus. On the other hand, Paul had changed and became a Sadducee courting and winning the support of the High Priest. Paul's relationship to Stephen is not actually spelled out in the New Testament but the record is very clear that Paul consented to the murder of Stephen. The evidence for Paul's complicity in this matter rests upon the fact that those who committed the murder laid their coats at the feet of Paul.

Paul was now secure in his relationship with the High Priest, so he began a systematic campaign against the followers of Jesus who were also known as the followers of THE WAY. The followers of THE WAY were those who believed that the written Mosaic law or the Torah should be discussed and reinterpreted from generation to generation. Paul would enter people's homes and drag off the 'men and women' and commit them to prison. (*Acts* 8: 3)

Paul was zealous in his persecution of the followers of Jesus. He went to the High Priest and asked him 'for letters to the synagogues at Damascus' where, if he found any 'belonging to THE WAY, men or women, he might bring them bound to Jerusalem' (*Acts* 9: 1-2).

As Paul was approaching Damascus he experienced an episode of conversion disorder. This is reported in the book of Acts.

> Now as he journeyed he approached Damascus, and suddenly a light from heaven flashed about him. And he fell to the ground and heard a voice saying to him, 'Paul, Paul why do you persecute me?' And he said, 'Who are you, Lord?' And he said, 'I am Jesus, whom you are persecuting; but rise, enter the city, and you will be told what you are to do.' The men who were travelling with him stood speechless, hearing the voice but seeing no one. (*Acts* 9: 3-7)

The agonizing death of Stephen and the subsequent persecution of the followers of Jesus carried out by Paul were surely active in his conscious mind. This would have been the case as he set off for Damascus. In addition to this Paul was acting against the wishes of his former teacher Gamaliel. Thus it is possible that the conflict between his very conscious persecutions and the now unconscious desires of his former teacher Gamaliel, became the unconscious conflict which led to his subsequent psychological trauma on the road to Damascus.

Paul's idea of resurrection was spiritual and not an actual flesh-and-blood body. Paul wrote: 'It is sown a physical body, it is raised a spiritual body' (*1 Cor.* 15: 44). Paul, however, has three references in his letters to his experience with the 'appearance' of Jesus. These references are: 1) *1 Cor.* 15: 8, 'Last of all, as one untimely born, he *appeared* also to me.' 2) *1 Cor.* 9: 1, 'Am I not free? Am I not an apostle? Have I not *seen* Jesus our Lord?' 3) *Gal* 1: 15-16, 'But when he who had set me apart before I was born, and had called me through his grace, was pleased to *reveal* his Son to me, in order that I might preach him to the Gentiles...' (Greek APOKALUPTO).

In the above three quotations from Paul's letters three different Greek words have been used for the English words 'appeared', 'seen', and 'revealed'. In *1 Cor.* 15: 8 the King James Version translates the Greek 'And last of all he was *seen* of me also...', but the Revised Standard Version translates the same passage 'Last of all, as one untimely born, he *appeared* also to me.' There is a great difference between seeing and appearing. To *see* implies that there is a mind-independent reality which is perceived. However, something may *appear* to a person which does not have a mind-independent reality.

In *1 Cor.* 9: 1 there is no difference between the translations in the King James Version and the Revised Standard Version. The King James Version is translated '... have I not *seen* Jesus Christ our Lord?' The Revised Standard Version keeps the same translation. Yet, the Greek word translated as 'see' is different from the word above which has been translated either 'appeared' or 'seen'.

In *Galatians* 1: 15-16 a different Greek word is used from the above two Greek words. This Greek word can be translated as 'to disclose' or 'to reveal' and both translations use the word 'reveal'. The King James Version, 'But when it pleased God... to reveal his son *in* me', is essentially the same as the Revised Standard Version 'But when he who had set me apart before I was born... was pleased to reveal his son *to* me...' Yet it is worth noting that the King James Version indicates that the Son was revealed *in* me where the Revised Standard Version indicates that the Son was revealed *to* me. (In a footnote in the *Oxford Annotated Bible* the editors indicate that the Greek actually means 'in'.)

I have given emphasis to the differences among Paul's own descriptions of what happened to him on the road because he was not clear whether the experience was in him or outside. This is important in attempting to identify the actual nature of his experience, that is, whether or not there was a mind-independent reality in his experience.

In the Acts of the Apostles there are three differing accounts of Paul's encounter with the resurrected Christ on the road to Damascus. The first is in *Acts* 9: 3-7.

Now as he journeyed he approached Damascus, and suddenly a light from heaven flashed about him. And he fell to the ground and heard a voice saying to him, 'Paul, Paul why do you persecute me? And he said, 'Who are you, Lord?' And he said, 'I am Jesus, whom you are persecuting; but rise, and enter the city, and you will be told what you are to do.' *The men who were travelling with him stood speechless, hearing the voice but seeing no one.* (My italics)

The second is in *Acts* 22: 6-11.

As I made my journey and drew near to Damascus, about noon a great light from heaven shone about me. And I fell to the ground and heard a voice saying to me, 'Paul, Paul, why do you persecute me?' And I answered, 'Who are you Lord?' And he said to me, 'I am Jesus of Nazareth whom you are persecuting.' Now *those* who were with me *saw the light* but *did not hear the voice* of the one who was speaking to me. (My italics)

The third is in *Acts* 26: 12.

Thus I journeyed to Damascus with the authority and commission of the chief priests. At midday, O King, *I saw on the way a light from heaven, brighter than the sun, shining round me and those who journeyed with me.*

There are major contradictions among these accounts. In *Acts* 9 the author wrote that those who were travelling with Paul stood speechless 'hearing the voice but seeing no one'. In *Acts* 22 those travelling with Paul 'saw the light but did not hear the voice'. In *Acts* 26 only Paul saw the light and heard the voice.

The above accounts vary from one another and it must be admitted that we can only guess what happened. Apparently Paul: 1) saw a bright light; 2) fell to the ground; 3) heard the voice of what he believed was Jesus; 4) might have had a vision of someone or something; 5) was blinded, and 6) recovered his sight three days later in Damascus.

At the time of this experience Paul was blinded; consequently, his companions led him 'by the hand and brought him into Damascus. And for three days he was without sight, and neither ate nor drank' (*Acts* 9: 1-9).

The Acts of the Apostles gives a very brief account of the role of Ananias and his visit to Paul. It is Ananias who was credited with the restoration of Paul's sight. So, what is known about Ananias?

In the Acts of the Apostles Ananias is referred to as:

... a devout man according to the law, well spoken of by all the Jews who lived there [Damascus], came to me, and standing by me said to me, 'Brother Paul, receive your sight.' And in that very hour I received my sight and saw him. And he said, 'The God of our fathers appointed you to know his will, to see the Just One and to hear a voice from his mouth; for you will be a witness for him to all men of what you have seen and heard. And now why do you wait? Rise and be baptized, and wash away your sins, calling on his name' (*Acts* 22: 12-16).

The very fact that this visit was recorded in Acts suggests that Ananias played a critical role in Paul's having regained his sight and having changed his religious direction. As already mentioned, there is a second account of this visit recorded in the Acts of the Apostles.

There was a disciple in Damascus named Ananias. He had a vision in which he heard the voice of the Lord: 'Ananias!' 'Here I am, Lord,' he answered. The Lord said to him, 'Go at once to Straight Street, to the house of Judas, and ask for a man from Tarsus named Paul. You will find him at prayer; he has had a vision of a man named Ananias coming in and laying his hands on him to restore his sight.' Ananias answered, *'Lord, I have often heard about this man and all the harm he has done to thy people in Jerusalem. And here he is with authority from the chief priests to arrest all who invoke thy name.'* But the Lord said to him, *'You must go, for this is my chosen instrument to bring my name before the nations and their kings, and before the people of Israel*; I myself will show him all that he must go through for my name's sake.' So Ananias went. He entered the house, laid his hands on him and said, 'Paul, my brother, the Lord Jesus, who appeared to you on your way here, *has sent me to you so that you may recover your sight*, and be filled with the Holy Spirit.' And immediately it seemed that scales fell from his eyes, and he regained his sight. Thereupon he was baptized, and afterwards he took food and his strength returned. (*Acts* 9: 10-19, my italics)

Again, it is hard for us today to imagine the strength and power of Paul's psychological trauma on the road. To Paul, it was not a psychological trauma but *a deep revelation from God*. When his sight returned and he recovered his strength, he built a new religious outlook based on this incident. He was now convinced that if Jesus of Nazareth spoke to him on the road then Jesus must have been resurrected by God, and if he was resurrected then he must have been the Messiah. (Messiah in Hebrew, Christos in Greek, and Christ in English.) Thus the concept of Jesus Christ was born.

He stayed some time with the disciples in Damascus. Soon he was proclaiming Jesus publicly in the synagogues: 'This,' he said, 'is the son of God.' All who heard him were astounded. 'Is not this the man', they said, 'who was in Jerusalem trying to destroy those who invoke his name? Did he not come here for the sole purpose of arresting them and taking them to the chief priests?' But Paul grew more forceful, and silenced the Jews of Damascus with his cogent proofs that Jesus was the Messiah. (*Acts* 9: 19-22)

It is clear from Paul's letter to the Galatians that the revelation on the road was the powerful fact which led to the development of a new religious outlook. Paul argued that he never learned his point of view from another human being. He said, 'I received it through a revelation of Jesus Christ' (*Gal*. 1: 11-12).

Prior to Paul's Damascus road experience he had been oriented externally to the enforcement of the law of Moses, or the Torah, which the larger society considered to be God's will. Following his psychological trauma he felt as though he had been liberated from Mosaic law, which had become an emotional strait-jacket for him. Paul wrote again and again about this very point, and it became the basis for what he called a new covenant. The evidence is as follows:

... our sufficiency is from God, who has qualified us to be ministers of a new covenant, *not in a written code but in the Spirit*, for the written code kills, but the Spirit gives life. (*2 Cor*. 3: 5-6, my italics)

Yes, to this day wherever Moses is read a veil lies over their minds; but when a man turns to the Lord the veil is removed. Now the Lord is the Spirit, and where the Spirit of the Lord is, there is freedom. (*2 Cor*. 3: 15)

... *if you are led by the spirit you are not under the law*... the fruit of the spirit is love, joy, peace, patience, kindness, goodness, faithfulness, gentleness, self-control; *against such there is no law*. (*Gal*. 5: 16-25, my italics)

Thus, Paul developed an awareness of different levels of consciousness within himself. His fundamental transition from an external, legal orientation which centred around the enforcement of Mosaic law, to an inner awareness of the importance of spirit, faith and love, led to the development of a new religious outlook for Paul.

On the one hand Paul often referred to himself, and on the other hand he would refer to 'Jesus Christ who is within me'. Henceforth, in his life, he distinguished between himself and an internal level of consciousness which he identified as Jesus Christ. This can be clearly seen in his writings; for example, in the administration of the communion service, Paul believed that he had received his instructions directly from Christ.

For I received from the Lord what I also delivered to you... (*1 Cor*. 11: 23)

We have seen that Paul mentioned having 'no word' from Christ:

> I have no commandment from the Lord, but I give my judgment as
> one who has obtained mercy of the Lord to be trustworthy. (*1 Cor.* 7:
> 25)

Paul joined the group in Damascus, and in a short period of time
he began to preach his new religion; however, in doing this he angered
innumerable people in Damascus, and it was rumoured that someone was going to kill him if he attempted to leave the city. Some of
his friends then lowered him down the wall in a basket and thus he
escaped. (*Acts* 9: 23-24)

Paul went into Arabia for three years. Some authorities believe that
he went to the Essene community where he lived and studied. (Wolfe,
p.330).

Following his stay in Arabia he returned to Jerusalem for his first
meeting with James and Peter. They were afraid of him because of
his former actions as a persecutor of the followers of Jesus. (Wolfe,
p.331)

The differences of opinion between Paul and James are classic.
James, Jesus' brother, was the leader of the Jerusalem community,
and he represented the Jewish dimension of the actual teachings of
Jesus. However, this point of view was of little interest to Paul, since
Paul believed he received his religious insights directly from the res-
urrected Jesus Christ through revelation.

Peter and James talked with Paul for fifteen days, and Paul refers
to this encounter in his letter to the Galatians.

> Then after three years I went up to Jerusalem to visit Cephas, and
> remained with him fifteen days. But I saw none other of the apostles,
> except James the Lord's brother. (In what I am writing to you, before
> God, I do not lie!) Then I went into the regions of Syria and Cilicia.
> (*Gal.* 1: 18-21)

It is remarkable that there is such correspondence between the book
of Acts, written by Luke, and Galatians which was written by Paul.
Perhaps this indicates that the author of the book of Acts had Paul's
letters before him when he wrote his book.

> And when he was come to Jerusalem, he attempted to join the disciples;
> but they were all afraid of him, not believing that he was a disciple.
> (*Acts* 9: 26)

Nothing has survived concerning the content of the conversations
which took place between these three men. Only slight intimations

are observable in Acts and Galatians regarding the 'tumultuous conflicts of that historic fortnight... Peter and James not only rejected Paul but also appear to have sent him home with the admonition that he refrain from any further ministry in the name of Jesus' (Wolfe, p.332). The brethren took Paul 'down to Caesarea and sent him forth to Tarsus' (*Acts* 9: 30).

Paul remained inactive in Tarsus for at least eight years until Barnabas went to visit him. Barnabas was impressed with Paul and persuaded Paul to accompany him to Antioch. Paul and Barnabas worked with the church in Antioch for at least a year.

And it came to pass that even for a whole year they were gathered together with the church, and taught many people, and that the disciples were called Christians first in Antioch. (*Acts* 11: 25-26)

Paul and Barnabas were asked by the members of the church in Antioch to take the money they had raised for famine relief to Jerusalem. This famine took place in the days of Claudius.

And the disciples determined, every one according to his ability, to send relief to the brethren who lived in Judea; and they did so, sending it to the elders by the hand of Barnabas and Paul. (*Acts* 11: 29-30)

About nine years later Paul made his second visit to Jerusalem, which was nearly as difficult as his first. Barnabas, however, was of great assistance to Paul.

Upon arrival in Jerusalem Paul and Barnabas apparently found Peter, James, and all the disciples as antagonistic toward him as the two leaders had been on the first visit... This time the bad reception was salvaged by Barnabas who 'took him and brought him to the apostles, and declared to them how he had seen the Lord in the way, and that he had spoken to him, and how he had preached boldly in the name of Jesus at Damascus' (Wolfe, p.334).

Paul was allowed to preach in Jerusalem on this visit but because of plots against his life he returned to Antioch. (The Hellenists mentioned in the following quotation were Jews who had a Greek background.)

So he went in and out among them at Jerusalem, preaching boldly in the name of the Lord. And he spoke and disputed against the Hellenists; but they were seeking to kill him. (*Acts* 9: 28-29)

Again Paul was in controversy in Antioch, so he and Barnabas were sent forth on a missionary journey.

Now in the church at Antioch there were prophets and teachers,

71

Barnabas, Symeon who was called Niger, Lucius of Cyrene, Manaen a member of the court of Herod the tetrarch, and Paul. While they were worshipping the Lord and fasting, the Holy Spirit said, 'Set apart for me Barnabas and Paul for the work to which I have called them.' Then after fasting and praying they laid their hands on them and sent them off. (*Acts* 13: 1-3)

Upon Paul's return to Antioch from his first missionary journey there continued to be disputes in the Antioch church. It was suggested that Paul and Barnabas should go to the leaders of the Jerusalem church and make peace. This resulted in the first ecumenical council of the Christian church. The meeting is described in *Acts* 15.

The dispute centred on the degree of compliance to Mosaic law that should be required of the Gentiles or non-Jews who were recruited into the church by Paul. According to the law of Moses every male should be circumcised, but Paul, in his mission to the uncircumcised or the Greeks, did not require compliance with this Mosaic law. In addition, Mosaic law required that the meat from any animal which had been sacrificed to an idol should not be eaten. Furthermore, every animal that was eaten should be killed in accordance with the ritual laid down in the law.

The compromise which was reached allowed Paul to recruit members, and they did not have to be circumcised. Yet, those who joined the church would be required to 'abstain from what has been sacrificed to idols' and only eat meat which had been killed ritually. They should also be chaste.

Following this meeting in Jerusalem Paul went on two more missionary journeys. Then Paul returned to Jerusalem where he met with a hostile reception. He was accused of teaching transgression of the law, and a major altercation ensued. Paul, in order to protect himself, appealed to Rome, which he was entitled to do as a Roman citizen. When he arrived in Rome he was kept under house arrest for two years. After his case was heard he was beheaded.

The *Oxford Dictionary of the Christian Church* summarizes Paul's life as follows:

St Paul is the most powerful human personality in the history of the church. From the decisive revelation on the way to Damascus his life was dominated by an ardent devotion to Christ, who was henceforward the centre both of his preaching and teaching and of his personal faith and life. (Cross and Livingstone, p.1047-8)

Verifying the Book of Acts from Paul's Letters

There are some New Testament scholars who point out that the book of Acts is a secondary source for information concerning the life of Paul, and it should be resolutely pushed aside. Lloyd Gaston, the distinguished New Testament scholar, wrote:

> ...Paul is to be interpreted strictly from his own writings and that the portrait of Paul to be found in the Acts and the Pastoral Epistles is to be put resolutely to one side. That is not to disparage the importance of the latter in their own right but only to adhere to the methodological principle that a primary source is always to be preferred to a secondary source. (Gaston, p.5)

Since many of the arguments used in this book are based on the book of Acts, it seems appropriate that an effort should be made to verify as much of the book of Acts as possible from the letters of Paul and from reliable contemporary scholars. This is a methodological procedure which Gaston does not follow and I believe his not following it has resulted in his making some major errors in interpretation.

There is another reason why it is important to verify the accuracy of the book of Acts from Paul's letters, since I have already argued that Paul's psychological experience on the road to Damascus was not, at base, either a 'religious conversion' or a 'call'. Generally, Paul's psychological experience on the road is looked at from a theological point of view; however, I have looked at Paul's emotional experience from a psychological or psychiatric point of view, and argued that he experienced conversion disorder which was caused by an emotional conflict as to whether he should or should not persecute the followers of Jesus. This experience, however, led him to make fundamental changes in his life.

Lloyd Gaston warns that '... a psychological approach has in the past led to serious misrepresentations.' Of course the reverse side of this argument is that ignoring the psychological interpretation might also lead to gross misrepresentations in the area of theological thought.

First, did Paul ever study under Gamaliel? In the New Testament the name of Gamaliel is only mentioned in the book of Acts; consequently, there is no way to confirm this point from the letters of Paul. We can, however, turn to modern scholars and see if they think that Paul had training in Jewish thought. If they think that he had

73

training, then it makes sense to accept the legend that he studied under Gamaliel. Norman Perrin reviewed the different arguments concerning Paul's education and came to the conclusion 'that one component in Paul's thought can be rooted in his Jewish background and education' (Perrin [1982], p.137). It makes sense to give credence to the legend that Paul studied under Gamaliel.

In reading Paul's letters I have traced all the major references to Jewish Scriptures (Old Testament), and he has relied very heavily on Genesis, Exodus, Leviticus, Numbers, Deuteronomy, I Samuel, I Kings, Job, Psalms, Proverbs, Isaiah, Jeremiah, Ezekiel and Hosea. As Paul built his own religious point of view, he has demonstrated his thorough knowledge and understanding of Jewish Scriptures by quoting from them in order to anchor his new point of view in previous Jewish thought. Yet it must be remembered that *all* his letters were written *after* his experience on the road to Damascus.

Second, some scholars have questioned the extent of persecution of the followers of Jesus, suggesting that the persecutions mentioned in the book of Acts have been exaggerated. We need to know whether these persecutions were or were not sponsored by the High Priests. This is very significant because Paul, if we are to believe Luke/Acts, became a party to these persecutions, and with the approval of the High Priest went to Damascus to persecute the followers of THE WAY.

E. P. Sanders, in his book *Jesus and Judaism*, wrote:

According to *Acts* 4: 5-22 Peter and John were arrested by the Jewish leaders, specifically by the chief priest and other members of the high priestly family (4: 6), on the ground of healing a man 'by the name of Jesus Christ of Nazareth' (4: 10). According to 5: 17-42 the High Priest and his colleagues (that is, Sadducees, as Luke tells us) arrested the apostles... Stephen was charged for speaking against the temple and the law. (6: 13) His speech (7: 2-53) indicates that the charge was at least justified, and he was stoned. (7: 57-60) Finally, we learn that Herod Agrippa I killed James, the son of Zebedee, and, finding that it pleased 'the Jews', also arrested Peter (12: 1-3)... There is one concrete piece of information about persecution in Josephus. When there was no procurator in Jerusalem, the High Priest had James, the brother of Jesus, executed... The second clear point is that the harassment of the Christians was at the instigation of the Jewish leadership. (Sanders, pp.284-285)

I also want to confirm whether Paul was present at the stoning to death of Stephen. Norman Perrin accepts the Luke/Acts reference to the presence of Paul at the stoning to death of Stephen. Perrin wrote:

According to Acts, Paul enters the early Christian scene as a bystander at the martyrdom of Stephen. (*Acts* 7: 58)

Perrin would like us to believe that Paul was a bystander at the stoning to death of Stephen. This seems quite unlikely since, if we can trust Luke/Acts, those who witnessed against Stephen went and laid their coats at the feet of Paul. If this reference is accepted then it is probable that Paul organized the whole incident and may have been responsible for the murder of Stephen.

The most persuasive evidence for the persecution of the followers of THE WAY comes from Paul himself:

You have heard what my manner of life was when I was still a practicing Jew: how *savagely* I persecuted the church of God, and *tried to destroy it*; and how in the practice of our national religion I was outstripping many of my Jewish contemporaries in my boundless devotion to the traditions of my ancestors. (*Gal.* 1: 13-14, my italics)

If anyone thinks to base his claims on externals, I could make a stronger case for myself: circumcised on the eighth day, Israelite by race, of the tribe of Benjamin, a Hebrew born and bred; in my attitude to the law, a Pharisee; in pious zeal a *persecutor* of the church; *in legal rectitude*, faultless. (*Phil.* 3: 4-6, my italics)

From these quotes we can grasp a clear feeling of the way Paul persecuted the followers of Jesus. It is important to remember that Paul was probably putting his behaviour in the best possible light because, as an apostle, it would have been wise to play down how he formerly persecuted the church.

It is clear that underneath these words lies a whole sub-layer of violence, which was in keeping with the persecutions of the church authorized by the High Priest. It is also quite certain that Paul was a leader in the horrors of persecution.

Third, we now come to Paul's psychological experience on the road to Damascus. Almost all authorities agree that Paul experienced a major psychological trauma of some kind. Norman Perrin has suggested that the author of Luke/Acts lays 'great weight' on Paul's Damascus road experience because the author relates the story three times. Perrin points out that the only constant element in the story as presented in Acts is the verbal exchange between Paul and the 'resurrected' Christ: 'Paul, Paul why do you persecute me?' 'Who are you Lord?' 'I am Jesus whom you are persecuting.' Perrin believes that embedded in the Damascus road experience is a 'vision' of Christ. (Perrin [1982], p.140)

Perrin raises a number of questions about the way in which this experience of Paul's should be interpreted. He wonders why Paul never expressed any guilt for his persecution of the followers of Jesus, and Perrin also wonders if the term 'conversion' is the appropriate one for Paul's experience. (Perrin [1982], p.139) Obviously Perrin is not comfortable with the idea of a religious conversion, but he does not suggest any other hypothesis in order to explain what happened to Paul.

Kirster Stendhal in his book *Paul among the Jews and Gentiles* has considerable difficulty with the 'conversion' of Paul. He proceeds to make a fundamental distinction between a 'conversion' and a 'call'. Stendhal believes that Paul was given a 'call' to take God's message to the Gentiles. Stendhal argues that as a Jew Paul was a persecutor of the followers of Jesus; yet, as a result of an overwhelming experience on the road to Damascus he abandons Judaism and becomes a Christian. Stendhal suggests that there was not a change of 'religion' which is commonly associated with a religious conversion. God's Messiah, Jesus Christ, only asks Paul to take God's message to the Gentiles. For Stendhal the emphasis is on the 'assignment' and not on 'conversion'. (Stendhal, p.7)

There are some crucial facts which Stendhal overlooks. There is no doubt that Paul's life was dramatically changed by his experience on the road to Damascus. However, it took some time for Paul to assimilate the full impact of his experience. It is very clear that the word 'Christians' was first used at Antioch many years following Paul's experience. We must also remember that the followers of Jesus were Jewish. Jesus was Jewish. Paul was Jewish, and the usual idea that Paul converted from one religion to another could not apply. In fact Paul's ideas led to the later development of what became Christianity. Stendhal has a problem with the concept of 'conversion'. He wants to gloss over the 'conversion experience' by giving emphasis to the concept of a 'call'. With regard to the 'call' Stendhal does not deal with the fact that Paul, in writing to the Thessalonians, wrote: '... for you suffered the same things from your own countrymen as they did from the Jews, who killed both the Lord Jesus and the prophets, and drove us out [from Judea].' If Paul was driven out of Judea *maybe he then wrote that he was called to the Gentiles* rather than admitting that he was not acceptable in Jerusalem. Yet, Stendhal cannot give up the fact that Paul had a 'deep' conversion experience of some kind. (Stendhal, p.12)

Once again we are fortunate because Paul himself writes of an experience[12] which happened to him; and this is one of the most important insights into Paul's life. Paul does not know what happened to him, and he states three times that only God knows the truth of this experience. Paul relates this incident:

> I must boast; there is nothing to be gained by it, but I will go on to visions and revelations of the Lord. *I know a man in Christ who fourteen years ago was caught up to the third heaven* – whether in the body or out of the body *I do not know, God knows.* And I know that *this man was caught up to the third heaven* – whether in the body or out of the body *I do not know. God knows.* And I know that this man was *caught up into Paradise* – whether in the body or out of the body *I do not know, God knows* – and he heard things that cannot be told, which man may not utter. On behalf of this man I will boast, but on my own behalf I will not boast, except of my weakness... *And to keep me from being too elated by the abundance of revelations,* a thorn was given to me in the flesh... (*2 Cor.* 12: 1-7, my italics)

In *The Oxford Annotated Bible* the editors make the following note about the above quote: '*I know a man,* an oblique reference to himself' (p.1405). From this reference in 2 Corinthians, I maintain that we can date, fairly closely, the time of Paul's trauma on the road to Damascus. The accepted date of Jesus' crucifixion is usually given as AD30. 2 Corinthians is dated around AD55. (Perrin [1982], p.181) If we subtract fourteen from fifty-five we end up dating Paul's trauma around AD41. (There could be a slight variation because none of the dates attributed to New Testament documents can be verified with exactitude.) Perrin suggests that Paul's conversion experience could have been as late as AD36. I argue that Paul's trauma occurred somewhere between AD36 and 41. The point here is not the exact date of this experience but to verify that it occurred, since its occurrence is denied by some scholars.

I have made an effort to establish the credibility of the book of Acts, and I contended that the Luke/Acts account is accurate as far as a major psychological experience is concerned because Paul writes of such an experience. My conclusion is in sharp contrast to the ideas as presented by Lloyd Gaston in his book *Paul and the Torah.* Concerning Paul, Gaston wrote: 'His call and commissioning as a revelation from God came while he was living in Damascus, not with the Lucan conversion fireworks but while quietly pondering the text of *Isaiah* 49, the second servant song' (Gaston, p.6). I do not know how Gaston could know that Paul was quietly pondering *Isaiah* 49.

77

However, the evidence in the book of Acts and in Paul's letters does not support Lloyd Gaston.

In my efforts to verify the major turning-points in Paul's life as they are presented in the book of Acts and at the same time verify the credibility of this book, there is one remaining point which helps in this process of confirmation. Did Paul escape from Damascus by having been let down the wall in a basket?

In the book of Luke/Acts we find the following quotation:

> As the days mounted up, the Jews hatched a plot against his [Paul's] life; but their plans became known to Paul. They kept watch on the city gates day and night so that they might murder him; but his converts took him one night and let him down the wall, lowering him in a basket. (*Acts* 9: 23-25)

In *2 Corinthians* 11: 31-33 we find a quote which confirms Paul's escape from Damascus. He wrote:

> The God and Father of the Lord Jesus Christ (blessed be his name for ever!) knows that what I say is true. When I was in Damascus, the commissioner of King Aretas kept the city under observation so as to have me arrested; and I was let down in a basket, through a window in the wall, and so escaped his clutches. (*2 Cor* 11: 31-33)

The following points have been confirmed either from the letters of Paul or they are points on which some authorities agree. These points are:

1. Paul was a student of rabbinical Judaism and this training must have been under a rabbi. I have assumed that he studied in Jerusalem under the liberal Pharisee Gamaliel.

2. The High Priests were persecuting the followers of Jesus, and Paul was a party to these persecutions. Paul was present at the stoning to death of Stephen. The evidence could indicate that he was responsible for the death. Paul admits that he savagely persecuted the followers of Jesus.

3. Most authorities agree that Paul had a deep psychological experience of some kind on the road to Damascus. In fact, most who grapple with this are baffled because they can only think of a 'religious conversion' or a 'call'. Yet, even Paul himself refers to a traumatic experience which he did not understand. I maintain that his experience occurred between AD36 and 41.

4. It has also been confirmed from Paul's letters that he escaped from Damascus by being let down the wall in a basket. This also tends to confirm the accuracy of Luke/Acts.

I believe that I have offered enough evidence from Paul's own letters and from contemporary authorities to justify my using the book of Acts in my analysis of Paul's experience on the road to Damascus. In the last chapter I argued that Paul's experience on the road was neither a 'call' nor a 'religious conversion' but was conversion disorder, which in itself gave rise to Paul's deep-felt belief in the 'resurrected' Christ.

Paul's Basic Religious Ideas

What were Paul's key ideas and how was his experience on the road to Damascus built into his new religious outlook? The central belief in Judaism was the oneness of God, and Paul never strayed from this fundamental conviction. In this theological sense he was Jewish until the end of his life. Paul believed that Jesus was raised from the dead by God but *Jesus was not God.*[13] This theological position is very clear in Paul's letters. In 1 Corinthians Paul wrote:

> ... and there is no God but one. (*1 Cor.* 8: 4)

> ... yet for us there is one God, the Father, from whom are all things and for whom we exist, and one Lord, Jesus Christ, through whom are all things and through whom we exist. (*1 Cor.* 8: 6)

Paul believed that the resurrected Jesus of Nazareth 'appeared' to him on the road to Damascus; thus, Jesus became the Messiah, or the Christ, and the turning-point in his new religious outlook. It was God who raised Jesus from the dead. In his letter to the Galatians Paul wrote:

> Paul an apostle, not from men or through man, but through Jesus Christ and God the Father, who raised him from the dead, and all the brethren who are with me... (*Gal.* 1: 1-2)

What was his concept of resurrection? He believed that Jesus was sown as a physical body and 'resurrected' as a spiritual body.

> But some will ask, 'How are the dead raised? With what kind of body do they come?' You foolish man! What you sow does not come to life unless it dies. And what you sow is not the body which is to be, but a bare kernel, perhaps of wheat or of some other grain. But God gives it a body as he has chosen, and to each kind of seed its own body... So it is with the resurrection of the dead. What is sown is perishable. It is sown in dishonour, it is raised in glory. It is sown in weakness, it is raised in power. *It is sown a physical body, it is raised a spiritual body*. If there is a physical body, there is also a spiritual

body... I tell you this, brethren: flesh and blood cannot inherit the Kingdom of God, nor does the perishable inherit the imperishable. (*1 Cor*. 15: 35-38, 42-44, 50, my italics)

Paul never argued for the presence of a flesh-and-blood body for the risen Christ. Christ's 'body' was spiritual.

Paul preached that, since Jesus Christ was and is a spiritual body, when you believe in him you will be in the spirit. In fact the values which are embodied in the flesh will die, and you yourself will be *resurrected* into the values of the spirit. Paul distinguished between being led by the spirit and doing the works of the flesh, or the works of the law. He wrote:

But I say, walk by the Spirit and do not gratify the desires of the flesh... But if you are led by the Spirit you are not under the law. Now the *works of the flesh* are plain: immorality, impurity, licentiousness, idolatry, sorcery, enmity, strife, jealousy, anger, selfishness, dissension, party spirit, envy, drunkenness, carousing, and the like... but *the fruit of the Spirit* is love, joy, peace, patience, kindness, goodness, faithfulness, gentleness, self-control; against such there is no law. And those who belong to Christ Jesus have crucified the flesh with its passions and desires. If we live in the Spirit, let us also walk in the Spirit. (*Gal*. 5: 16-25, my italics)

Paul founded his churches on the passionate belief that Jesus was 'resurrected' from the dead, that Jesus Christ appeared to him, and if one believed in Christ Jesus one would be a new creation and have eternal life. Good works would come into your life as a result of faith in Jesus Christ.

Paul wrote:

But by your hard and impenitent heart you are storing up wrath for yourself on the day of wrath when God's righteous judgment will be revealed. For he will render to every man according to his works: to those who by patience in well-doing seek for glory and honour and immortality, he will give eternal life; but for those who are factious and do not obey the truth, but obey wickedness, there will be wrath and fury... but glory and honour and peace for everyone who does good, the Jew first and also the Greek, for God shows no partiality. (*Rom*. 2: 5-8)

Paul developed a religion which was many-sided. At times, he gave emphasis to the importance of love:

So faith, hope, love abide, these three; but the greatest of these is love. (*1 Cor*. 13: 13)

Following Paul's psychological experience on the road to Damascus, he believed that he had direct communication with God through the 'resurrected' Jesus Christ. He wrote:

Therefore, if any one is in Christ, he is a new creation; the old has passed away, behold, the new has come. All this is from God, who through Christ reconciled us to himself and gave us the ministry of reconciling the world to himself... (2 Cor. 5: 17-18)

In this chapter a brief account of the life of the apostle Paul has been presented. Key points in the book of Acts have been verified by referring to Paul's letters or to contemporary scholars. In addition Paul's religious ideas have been briefly outlined.

In the next chapter I will review a debate between two well-known philosophers. They are Dr Antony Flew and Dr Gary Habermas. They debated whether Jesus was or was not literally resurrected from the dead.

I am reviewing this debate because it is an opportunity to show how the ideas presented in this book would have made it possible for the debate to have been much sharper than it was. On the one hand, Dr Flew was absolutely correct in the position which he took but he, at that time, was unable to offer a naturalistic explanation for the central events in the New Testament. Thus he lost the debate.

On the other hand, Dr Gary Habermas argued that Mary Magdalene, the disciples and Paul had experiences of some kind; but Dr Habermas, in the course of the debate, argued that the hallucination theory had been thoroughly discredited.

If the two hypotheses suggested in my book are taken seriously there is ample evidence in the New Testament for grief-related hallucinations and conversion disorder. Reviewing this debate gives me an opportunity to show how a new psychological approach to the material contained in the New Testament can give us a much clearer idea of what might have happened in the first century of our era.

Chapter 6

The Habermas-Flew Debate:
Arguments For and Against
the Resurrection of Jesus

Dr Gary R Habermas[14] and Dr Antony G N Flew,[15] both scholars of international reputation, engaged in a widely publicized debate[16] at Liberty University, Texas, in 1985. The text of their debate was published in Habermas and Flew's book *Did Jesus Rise from the Dead?*

Dr W David Beck, Chairman, Department of Philosophy of Liberty University, wrote the preface to the book in which he suggested that 'the Resurrection of Jesus Christ is the most significant topic of our day' (Habermas and Flew, ix). Dr Beck pointed out that Habermas is an expert on the historical evidence supporting the resurrection, and Flew is an expert on the impossibility of miracles. Thus, a meaningful debate was possible. (Habermas and Flew, ix)

Dr Habermas and Dr Flew agreed that the question of the resurrection must be settled on the basis of the sufficiency of the evidence which is contained in the New Testament.

At the end of the debate two panels of experts voted for the winner. One panel consisted of five distinguished philosophers, and the other consisted of five professional debate judges.

The overall decision of the two panels, judging both content and argumentation technique, 'was a seven-to-two decision (with one draw) in favour of the historicity of the Resurrection as argued by Habermas' (Habermas and Flew, xv).

The Debate

The two debaters agreed upon three fundamentals:

First, we both construe RESURRECTION, or rising from the dead, in a thoroughly literal and physical way...

Second, we are again agreed that the question whether, in that literal understanding, Jesus did rise from the dead is of supreme theoretical and practical importance.

Third, we are agreed both that identification is the defining and distinguishing characteristic of the true Christian, and that it is scarcely possible to make it without also accepting that the Resurrection did literally happen. (Habermas and Flew, p.3)

Flew's argument against the resurrection is divided into two parts:

The first deals with the general difficulty, perhaps impossibility, of establishing the occurrence of a miracle so as to be the foundation of a system of religion. The second turns to the inadequacies of the evidence actually available in the present case. (Habermas and Flew, p.4)

Flew's general argument against a miracle flows from David Hume's FIRST ENQUIRY, which asserts that the evidence required to establish the genuinely miraculous has to be much stronger than that needed to prove the highly unusual or the merely marvellous. The essence of Flew's philosophical argument against the resurrection is as follows:

The heart of the matter is that the criteria by which we must assess historical testimony, and the general presumptions that make it possible for us to construe leftovers from the past as historical evidence, are such that the possibility of establishing, on purely historical grounds, that some genuinely miraculous event has occurred is ruled out. (Habermas and Flew, p.5)

Flew further contends that the evidence concerning the resurrection presented in the New Testament is contradictory and is not strong enough to support the occurrence of a genuine miracle.

He points out, for example, that Paul lists the first appearance of Christ as having been to Peter, while the Gospels report that the first appearance was made to Mary Magdalene. Paul talks of a spiritual body, yet the Gospels give emphasis to a flesh-and-blood body which can be touched. Flew suggests that *'to the unsanctified eye, however, seeing spiritual bodies is indiscernible from having visions to which no mind-independent realities correspond'* (my italics, Habermas and Flew, p.11).

Flew's general conclusion is:

In fact, in view of these and many other deficiencies in the materials available, my own conviction is that we have no chance either of developing a modestly acceptable outline account of what actually happened in Jerusalem during that original Easter weekend, or of determining how or when believers first came to believe that on the third day Jesus physically rose from the dead.

Be that as it may; for in order to warrant disbelief, none of that is necessary. It is only sufficient to show that no evidence has been presented so strong as to call for a radical shake-up of the ordinary presuppositions of critical history. We have no alternative but to continue in the presumption that anything that is accepted as being naturally impossible did not happen. (Habermas and Flew, p.11)

Gary Habermas presented the arguments in support of the resurrection, and won the debate because he offered a series of historical facts and then argued that, in the absence of any naturalistic explanation for these facts, *the resurrection hypothesis must be accepted.*

Habermas outlined eleven events in the New Testament that are considered to be knowable history by virtually all contemporary New Testament scholars, and a twelfth event considered to be knowable history by many scholars. These twelve points are:

(1) Jesus died due to the rigours of crucifixion, and (2) was buried. (3) Jesus' death caused the disciples to despair and lose hope. (4) Although not as frequently recognized, many scholars hold that Jesus was buried in a tomb that was discovered to be empty just a few days later.

Critical scholars even agree that (5) *at this time the disciples had real experiences that they believed were literal appearances of the risen Jesus.* Because of these experiences, (6) the disciples were transformed from doubters, who were afraid to identify themselves with Jesus, to bold proclaimers of his death and resurrection, even willing to die for this belief. (7) This message was central in the early church preaching and (8) was especially proclaimed in Jerusalem, where Jesus had died shortly before.

As a result of this message, (9) the church was born and grew, (10) with Sunday as the primary day of worship. (11) James, the brother of Jesus and a sceptic, was converted to the faith when he also believed he saw the resurrected Jesus. (12) A few years later *Paul, the persecutor of Christians, was also converted by an experience that he, similarly, believed to be an appearance of the risen Jesus.*

These historical facts are crucial to a contemporary investigation of Jesus' Resurrection. Except for the empty tomb, virtually all critical scholars who deal with this issue agree that these are the minimum known historical facts regarding this event. Any conclusion concerning the historicity of the Resurrection should therefore properly account for this data. *The pivotal fact, recognized as historical by virtually all scholars, is the original experiences of the disciples. It is nearly always admitted that the disciples had actual experiences and that something really happened.* Interestingly, varying critical positions that support the literal facticity of Jesus' Resurrection are currently popular. (Habermas and Flew, pp.19-20, my italics)

Out of these twelve facts Habermas selects the original experiences of the disciples as pivotal.

Habermas goes on to examine four sets of arguments for the resurrection. His summary statements are:

First, naturalistic theories have failed to explain away this event, chiefly because each theory is disproved by the known historical facts. (Habermas and Flew, p.20)

The key evidence for Jesus' Resurrection is (1) the disciples' eyewitness experiences, which they believed to be literal appearances of the risen Jesus; these experiences have not been explained by naturalistic theories and additional facts corroborate this eyewitness testimony. (Habermas and Flew, p.22)

At any rate, the Gospel accounts of the Resurrection (and the earliest reports included in them, in particular) should be utilized as records of what the eyewitnesses actually saw. For reasons such as these, many, if not most, critical theologians hold either that the literal event of the Resurrection can be accepted by faith *or that some sort of literal appearances (abstract or bodily) may be postulated as historical realities.* (Habermas and Flew, p.24, my italics)

We have already made a thorough investigation into the evidence which is contained in the New Testament.

Response to the Habermas-Flew Debate

In the above the substance of the Gary Habermas and Antony Flew debate is presented. Habermas won the debate because Flew offered 'no plausible naturalistic evidence against' the resurrection of Jesus. Flew was unable to refute Habermas' argument that:

The key evidence for Jesus' resurrection is (1) *the disciples' eyewitness experiences, which they believed to be literal appearances of the risen Jesus; these appearances have not been explained by naturalistic theories...* (Habermas and Flew, p.22, my italics)

I have presented two naturalistic explanations in this book. I have argued that the myth of the Resurrection, the Ascension and the Pentecost arose out of the normal grief-related hallucinations of Mary Magdalene and the disciples which they, erroneously, interpreted as physical appearances of Jesus. I have argued that the apostle Paul's belief in the 'resurrected' Christ arose because he felt united with the 'resurrected' Christ, and this arose from the mystical dimension of his episode of conversion disorder. I believe this generated Paul's myth of the resurrected Jesus Christ.

I will now respond to the Habermas-Flew debate.

The two debaters agreed on three fundamental propositions:

1) *They both construed resurrection, or rising from the dead, in a thoroughly literal and physical way.* There are many Christians who would not agree with this first proposition. In fact we have already seen that Paul would not have agreed with this starting-point. Paul insisted that Jesus was buried a physical body and he was resurrected a spiritual body. For the sake of argument, however, I will proceed with the conditions laid down in the debate.

2) *Whether Jesus did or did not rise from the dead in a thoroughly physical way is the only reason for accepting or not accepting Jesus as the God of Abraham, Isaac, and Israel.* There is not a shred of evidence in the New Testament to support the idea that Jesus was considered to be God. Paul was absolutely clear that there was a sharp distinction between God and Jesus. According to Paul, God raised Jesus from the dead but Jesus was not God. Also, the only reference to the Trinitarian formula in the Gospels was a later insertion into the text.

3) *In order to be a true Christian one must accept the literal and physical resurrection of Jesus of Nazareth.* Once again the first person who objected to this point of view was Paul.

Flew's first argument against the resurrection was based on the proposition that there is not sufficient reliable historical evidence ever to establish the historicity of the resurrection.

In our review of the evidence in the Gospels we sustained Flew's historical argument. We discovered that there was no person in the Gospel accounts who actually witnessed a physical resurrection of Jesus of Nazareth, that is, there was no one who verified that Jesus was actually dead and then witnessed God's actual resurrection of the dead body. Flew's argument that the evidence does not support the physical resurrection of Jesus of Nazareth on the basis of the Gospel accounts is correct.

Flew's second attack on the doctrine of the Resurrection stems from his contention that the evidence in the New Testament contains great flaws and contradictions and therefore cannot support the idea of the physical resurrection of Jesus Christ.

Once again, Flew is absolutely correct. He uses the Birth stories in the Gospels to show how previous ideas contained in Jewish scriptures influenced the way in which the story of Jesus' birth was written. In addition he showed the many contradictions in the birth stories. His point is that the records, when looked at from the point of view of critical history, are unreliable.

Flew also showed the contradictions between Paul's letters and the Gospels. Paul reported that Jesus first appeared to Peter, while the Gospels reported that Jesus first appeared to Mary Magdalene. Flew's arguments were very sound and sustained his argument that the evidence for a miracle must be airtight but the New Testament records are so contradictory that they cannot support the doctrine of the Resurrection of Jesus of Nazareth.

Gary Habermas, on the other hand, won the debate because he offered twelve historical points and then suggested that, in the absence of a naturalistic explanation for these historical points, the only hypothesis which explains these facts is the physical resurrection of Jesus of Nazareth.

Habermas' twelve historical points (of which eleven are well-accepted though the tradition of the empty tomb remains in dispute) are better explained by my two hypotheses of conversion disorder and bereavement. These two hypotheses will account for all twelve historical facts, including the 'tomb' story.

I will now give consideration to each one of Habermas' twelve points. In this debate Habermas has placed the information presented in the Gospels before that of Paul. In our inquiries into the New Testament we noted that Paul's letters were written before the Gospels. I believe Habermas should have made it clear that the Gospels, in some respects, reflect the ideas which were already developed by Paul.

In spite of this, however, we will proceed with his twelve points. (Each of his twelve points is in capital letters.)

(1) JESUS DIED DUE TO THE RIGOURS OF CRUCIFIXION.

One of the strongest arguments supporting the crucifixion is the fact that the bereavement patterns of Mary Magdalene and the disciples were absolutely normal. What happened to them could not have happened if there had not been a traumatic death which was of great personal meaning to them.

(2) AND WAS BURIED.

It is not clear to critical scholars where Jesus was buried. The thesis that Mary Magdalene and the disciples experienced grief following the crucifixion of Jesus of Nazareth does not depend on the place of burial. That is, wherever they went they would have experienced grief.

(3) JESUS' DEATH CAUSED THE DISCIPLES TO DESPAIR AND LOSE HOPE.

This is an absolutely normal grief experience. The first phase in bereavement is to be plunged into despair, sadness and loneliness. As acute grief sets in they would have experienced anger, denial, anxiety, guilt and general tension. These are normal grieving experiences.

(4) ALTHOUGH NOT AS FREQUENTLY RECOGNIZED, MANY SCHOLARS HOLD THAT JESUS WAS BURIED IN A TOMB THAT WAS DISCOVERED TO BE EMPTY JUST A FEW DAYS LATER.

It must be recognized that in the entire New Testament there was no witness to a physical resurrection of Jesus of Nazareth. However, one of the main arguments for the 'resurrection' of Jesus was the 'evidence' of the empty tomb.

Whether Jesus was buried in a tomb or not makes absolutely no difference to the disciples' belief that he was resurrected, because they were experiencing grief. Furthermore, using the argument of an empty tomb as evidence for resurrection is absurd since the historical records are not accurate enough to rule out the possibility that the body was removed by natural means. Maybe Jesus' friends or enemies came and removed the body.

More than likely, however, Jesus' body was thrown into the place of 'the skull' which would have been common practice at that time. This is explained by the Anglican Bishop Barnes:

> After the crucifixion of Jesus they (the followers of Jesus) were scattered fugitives, followers of a man who came to a criminal's end, whose body quite possibly had been flung ignominiously into a common malefactor's grave. (Barnes, p.174)

Bishop John Shelby Spong also writes that in his opinion Jesus was probably buried in a common grave and not in a tomb.

> He died the death of a publicly executed criminal. His body probably received the typical treatment given to those so unfortunate as to fall into that category. He was removed from the instrument of execution, placed into a common grave, and covered over. (Spong, p.241)

Even if the empty tomb story might be true, it is far more plausible to theorize that the body was removed by human rather than 'divine' hands. At any rate an empty tomb story is irrelevant to the argument which is presented in this book.

(5) CRITICAL SCHOLARS EVEN AGREE THAT AT THIS TIME THE DISCIPLES HAD REAL EXPERIENCES THAT THEY BELIEVED WERE LITERAL APPEARANCES OF THE RISEN JESUS:

The second argument for the 'resurrection' of Jesus has always been the reports of appearances of Jesus to Mary Magdalene and the disciples. However, I have argued that as a consequence of Jesus' death, Mary Magdalene and the disciples were experiencing very normal grief-related hallucinations.

Mary Magdalene was grieving the loss of her leader – Jesus. Apparitions are frequently experienced by those who were closest to the recently deceased. This has been carefully documented by contemporary grief research. On this theory it is to be expected that Mary Magdalene might have seen vivid appearances or apparitions of Jesus. The Gospels report that she did have apparitions of Jesus which she believed to be actual 'physical' appearances of the 'resurrected' Jesus of Nazareth. If these apparitions actually occurred they are attributable to symptoms of severe grief and cannot be used as arguments for the physical resurrection of Jesus of Nazareth. When Mary reported these grief-related hallucinations to the disciples they did not believe her.

Peter and James are reported to have experienced 'appearances' in *I Cor.* 15: 5, 7. Grieving is not over in an hour or two, or even in a few days or weeks; consequently, wherever the disciples went, whether to Galilee or Jerusalem, they took their grief with them.

On the basis of grief theory it is quite logical to assume that all of Jesus' close followers might have experienced apparitions or any one of the five hallucinations which are common in grief. It would have been logical that Peter would have been one to experience apparitions of Jesus, since Peter had denied knowing him. This must have caused him considerable guilt as events unfolded. James was Jesus' brother. Again his stress would have been extreme as he watched his brother die on the cross. On the theory that those who experience apparitions are usually those who are closest to the deceased, it would be quite logical that James could have seen an apparition of his brother. Apparitions constitute evidence for grief and not for resurrection.

It must also be mentioned that many of the disciples denied having seen Jesus in some of their group meetings, so Paul's report, years later, of the appearances to the twelve and the apostles remains very much in doubt. Nevertheless, it is possible for groups to experience collectively the illusion of the presence of the deceased.

Since these stories were told and retold over a period of forty to seventy years following their occurrence, they would surely have been magnified in order to support a new theological position. However, it has already been noted that every appearance story contains within it a core grief-related hallucination which, today, is considered to be normal.

> (6) BECAUSE OF THESE EXPERIENCES, THE DISCIPLES WERE
> TRANSFORMED FROM DOUBTERS, WHO WERE AFRAID TO IDENTIFY
> THEMSELVES WITH JESUS, TO BOLD PROCLAIMERS OF HIS DEATH
> AND RESURRECTION, EVEN WILLING TO DIE FOR THIS BELIEF.

This, once again, is a very normal bereavement pattern, especially when the deceased was a prophet or a charismatic leader who has been executed. The myth or legend contained in the Acts of the Apostles suggests that the impact of Jesus remained emotionally active in the psychological structure of the disciples over a forty-day period, as they attempted to come to grips with this devastating and tragic event. The women and the disciples recovered their internal sense of self-possession on the fortieth day, and then on the fiftieth day they began their lives with new commitment and direction. This renewal of life is absolutely normal in bereavement.

The disciples accepted their loss. They acquired new behavioural dispositions and relationships. They reorganized their lives, and when they decided what they were going to do on the fortieth day, they externalized this turning-point into the myth of the Ascension. On the fiftieth day they began their new way of life with a new and deeper sense of dedication. Thus they took on a new level of commitment. This new energy level was externalized into the myth of the Pentecost or the descent of the Holy Spirit. All of this is the very significant externalization of a rather normal bereavement pattern.

This renewal of commitment and energy is normal in bereavement and is not dependent upon the concept of the 'physical resurrection' of Jesus of Nazareth.

> (7) THIS MESSAGE WAS CENTRAL IN THE EARLY CHURCH
> PREACHING.

In item (6) Habermas asserts that the followers of Jesus became bold proclaimers of Jesus' death and resurrection. Habermas further asserts that the disciples were willing to die for this belief.

This second assertion on the part of Habermas ignores the complex political and religious situation in Jerusalem at the time of Jesus' death, and this has led Habermas to make a major error. The error is that the disciples were not executed because of their belief in the resurrection of Jesus of Nazareth but because they were perceived as having been a political threat to both the Sadducees and the ruling Roman authorities.

This point of view has been clearly explained by Hyam Maccoby in his book *The Mythmaker:*

> Since Jesus certainly came into conflict with the High Priest of his day, who was a Sadducee, it would be quite natural for stories to be preserved in which Jesus figures as an opponent of Sadducee religious doctrines, even though, as we shall see, the *chief* point of conflict between Jesus and the Sadducees was political rather than religious. In the Pharisee literature many stories are found about Pharisee teachers who engaged in argument with Sadducees. A frequent topic of these debates was the question of the resurrection of the dead, in which the Pharisees believed, and the Sadducees disbelieved. As it happens, such a story has been preserved in the Gospels about Jesus (*Mark* 12: 18-27 and parallels). The answers given to the Sadducees by Jesus are typical of those given by Pharisees in their debates. Even among non-Jews it was too well known that the Pharisees believed in resurrection for these stories to be re-edited as confrontations between Jesus and the Pharisees, so they were left unaltered – interesting evidence of the status of Jesus as a Pharisee, though, of course, the Gospels represent Jesus as arguing, not as a Pharisee, but simply as one whose views happen for once to coincide with those of the Pharisees.
>
> What was the motive for the re-editing of stories about conflict between Jesus and the Sadducees so that he was portrayed as in conflict with the Pharisees instead? The reason is simple. The Pharisees were known to be the chief religious authorities of the Jews, not the Sadducees. In fact, at the time that the Gospels were edited, the Sadducees had lost any small religious importance that they had once had, and the Pharisees were the sole repository of religious authority. As we shall see shortly in more detail, it was of the utmost importance to the Gospel editors to represent Jesus as having been a rebel against Jewish religion, not against the Roman occupation. (Maccoby, pp.34-35)

Gamaliel was the leading Pharisee in Jerusalem following the death of Jesus. In Gamaliel's speech to the Sanhedrin he was the one who argued that the followers of Jesus should not be persecuted.

The followers of Jesus were not persecuted because they believed in the resurrection of Jesus of Nazareth. Rather, they were persecuted because they were perceived, by the High Priest, to be a political threat to both the Sadducees and the Romans.

(8) THIS MESSAGE WAS ESPECIALLY PROCLAIMED IN JERUSALEM, WHERE JESUS HAD DIED SHORTLY BEFORE.

The Jerusalem church was under the leadership of James, and James and Paul did not agree. The most successful evangelist was Paul through his mission to other parts of the Roman empire.

(9) AS A RESULT OF THIS MESSAGE THE CHURCH WAS BORN AND GREW...

The church was born and did grow, but its growth was outside Jerusalem. The Romans destroyed Jerusalem in AD70 and the small Jewish Christian group in Jerusalem was scattered.

The churches which survived were those established by Paul, and they were outside Jerusalem.

(10) ... WITH SUNDAY AS THE PRIMARY DAY OF WORSHIP.

Habermas does not indicate the true significance of this point; however, it is true that over a period of time the Christian day of worship shifted from the seventh day to the first day.

This is explained in George Stimpson's book *A Book about the Bible*:

> Adoption of Sunday as the Christian Sabbath was gradual. SUNDAY, which occurs nowhere in the Bible, is derived from Anglo-Saxon SUNNANDAEG, 'day of the sun', the first day of the week having been dedicated to the sun by the pagans. The commandment, 'Remember the Sabbath day, to keep it holy', referred to the ancient Jewish Sabbath, which was the seventh day of the week according to the Hebrew calendar. That the New Testament writers clearly distinguished between the Sabbath and the first day of the week is shown by several passages in which the first day is mentioned as following the Sabbath. Although Jesus himself observed the Sabbath, St Paul seems to have placed observance of this day among the customs not obligatory on Christians. 'Let no man therefore,' he says in *Colossians* 2: 16, 'judge you in meat, or in drink or in respect of an holy day, or of the new moon, or of the Sabbath days.' ...Whatever the true meaning of these passages, from the beginning many of the Christians commemorated the first day of the week as Resurrection day, the day on which Jesus rose from the dead. (Stimpson, p.96)

(11) JAMES, THE BROTHER OF JESUS AND A SCEPTIC, WAS

CONVERTED TO THE FAITH WHEN HE ALSO BELIEVED HE SAW
THE RESURRECTED JESUS.

James, Jesus' brother, became the leader of the Jerusalem church
following the death of Jesus. It is to be noted that James was neither
an apostle nor a disciple. He became the leader because he was Jesus'
brother.

Protestants, however, as well as most independent scholars, generally believe that James, Joses, Simon and Judas, and *his sisters* mentioned in *Matthew* 13: 55, were blood brothers and sisters who were
born to Mary and Joseph after the birth of Jesus. Several references
in the epistles of Paul and in Acts are the basis of the accepted belief
that after the crucifixion of Jesus his brother James succeeded to the
leadership of the Christian community in Jerusalem. The idea of
family succession was so firmly established that it is likely that the
followers of Jesus assumed that his next oldest brother alone would
be worthy to succeed him as the head of the new Jewish sect. (Stimpson, pp.34-35)

In the Gospels, however, there is no record of James having
experienced an apparition of Jesus. The only reference to James'
having seen the 'resurrected' Christ is contained in one of Paul's letters (*1 Cor*. 15: 7). If James did see an apparition of Jesus it would
have been logical, since those who were closest to the deceased were
the ones who would have been most likely to experience apparitions.

(12) A FEW YEARS LATER , PAUL, THE PERSECUTOR OF CHRISTIANS,
WAS ALSO CONVERTED BY AN EXPERIENCE THAT HE, SIMILARLY,
BELIEVED TO BE AN APPEARANCE OF THE RISEN JESUS.

I have argued that Paul's experience on the road to Damascus might
have occurred somewhere between AD38 and AD41. Paul's experience
must be distinguished from the experiences of Mary Magdalene and
the disciples.

Paul, however, suffered conversion disorder, and a normal accompaniment of this psychological trauma can be a loss of motor coordination, the hearing of voices, the seeing of lights, visions and
blindness. All of these symptoms were experienced by Paul. Conversion disorder can come on instantly and can leave instantly. This
whole psychological phenomenon is not under voluntary control;
therefore, Paul believed that Jesus of Nazareth was resurrected and
presented to him by God.

Conversion disorder can also cause the person who has the experience to feel that he has been united with a higher power. (Mayer-Gross, p.134) In Paul's case this unification experience centred around the voice of what he believed was the voice of Jesus. This led him to believe that he had encountered the 'resurrected' Jesus Christ.

The correct response to Habermas is, therefore, that the twelve historical facts can be naturally explained by giving serious consideration to the hallucinations which accompany bereavement and the psychological symptoms which accompany conversion disorder.

Chapter 7

The Religious Dimension of Paul's Jesus Christ

Why was Paul's new religious emphasis so important that he became the real founder of Christianity? This question is extremely important and I will propose an answer: Paul gave emphasis to a theory of resurrection which, if believed, would alleviate the believer's anxiety concerning death. Inadvertently, Paul was forced, through his belief that he had been united with the resurrected Jesus Christ, to confront the death of Jesus of Nazareth and to give a 'rational' explanation for his having heard the voice of Jesus. Of course, he had no way of knowing that the hearing of voices could be a normal symptom of conversion disorder since conversion disorder has only been fully understood in this century through and following the work of Sigmund Freud. Paul, however, reasoned that since Jesus spoke to him on the road then Jesus must have been 'resurrected'. Furthermore, since he, Paul, did not voluntarily bring on this experience then it must have been a revelation from God. In this way God had chosen him for a special mission. As this viewpoint matured it was radically different from that of his contemporaries.

Consequently, Paul wrote that the 'resurrection' of Jesus Christ was an act of God and Jesus Christ was revealed to him by God. He did not learn about the 'resurrection' from any other person. Paul then began to develop a theological system focused on death and resurrection, including the idea that those who believed in Jesus Christ would also have eternal life. This theory addresses every believer's existential anxiety concerning death.

Norman Perrin wrote concerning the death and 'resurrection' of Jesus of Nazareth or the Christ-event: 'The "Christ-event" is a "creative act," a foundational "myth," which gives meaning and purpose to human existence in the world' (Perrin [1982], p.197).

95

The New Testament contains seven letters which are attributed to Paul. Since Paul's letters were so very influential in the formation of the early Christian churches we have, fortunately, an excellent record of what Paul thought and what he taught.

I will review Paul's letters and extract from them the dominant themes discussed by him.

Paul's most important and bedrock theme was his deeply felt and absolute faith that Jesus of Nazareth was 'resurrected' from the dead by God and thus became Jesus Christ. This 'resurrection' was an act of God since he, Paul, never solicited his confrontation with the 'risen' Christ. Consider the following:

> It will be reckoned to us who believe in him [God] that raised from the dead Jesus our Lord, who was put to death for our trespasses and raised for our justification. (*Rom.* 4: 24)

> We were buried therefore with him by baptism into death, so that as Christ was raised from the dead by the glory of the Father, we too might walk in newness of life. (*Rom.* 6: 4)

> If the Spirit of him [God] who raised Jesus from the dead dwells in you, he who raised Christ Jesus from the dead will give life to your mortal bodies also through his [God's] Spirit which dwells in you. (*Rom.* 8: 11)

The next theme in Paul's new religion is that belief in Jesus Christ will result in personal resurrection and eternal life for the believer. This is a second and dominant theme in the history of Christianity. This is the belief which will allay the believer's personal anxiety concerning death.

In *1 Thessalonians* we find the following:

> For since we believe that Jesus died and rose again, even so, through Jesus, God will bring with him those who have fallen asleep. (4: 14)

> And the dead in Christ will rise first; then we who are alive, who are left, shall be caught up together with them in the clouds to meet the Lord in the air; and so we shall always be with the Lord. Therefore comfort one another with these words. (4: 16-18)

> For God has not destined us for wrath, but to obtain salvation through our Lord Jesus Christ, who died for us so that whether we wake or sleep we might live with him. (5: 9)

In *1 Corinthians* Paul wrote:

> And God raised the Lord and will also raise us up by his power. (6: 14)

But in fact Christ has been raised from the dead, the firstfruits of those who have fallen asleep, for as by a man came death, by a man has come also the resurrection of the dead. For as in Adam all die, so also in Christ shall all be made alive. (15: 20)

It is sown a physical body, it is raised a spiritual body. If there is a physical body, there is also a spiritual body. (15: 44)

In *2 Corinthians* the same theme is dominant:

But it is God who establishes us with you in Christ... (1: 21)

... knowing that he who raised the Lord Jesus will raise us also with Jesus and bring us with you into his presence. (4: 14)

Therefore, if any one is in Christ, he is a new creation; the old has passed away, behold, the new has come. All this is from God, who through Christ reconciled us to himself... (5: 17-19)

In Paul's letter to the Romans this theme still remains dominant:

It will be reckoned to us who believe in him [God] that raised from the dead Jesus our Lord, who was put to death for our trespasses and raised for our justification. (*Rom.* 4: 24-25)

... the free gift of God is eternal life in Christ Jesus our Lord. (6: 22)

For the law of the Spirit in Christ Jesus has set me free from the law of sin and death... If the Spirit of him who raised Jesus from the dead dwells in you, he who raised Christ Jesus from the dead will give life to your mortal bodies also through his Spirit which dwells in you. (8: 2, 11)

Paul developed and preached a theory or belief system of resurrection which was based on the mystical dimension of his episode of conversion disorder. In this way he addressed the existential anxiety surrounding death which confronts every thinking human being, and his firm faith in the 'resurrected' Christ allayed his anxiety concerning his own death. This was a powerful experience for Paul and his system remains at the centre of Christianity to the present time.

The question must now be raised as to the reason why this message was so powerful to the people of his time? Those of us who live in industrial society have very little feeling for the oppressive dominance of death as it existed in pre-industrial society.

Consider the following: If in any given year, in the first century, there were 100 live births, within six years 33 of the infants would be dead. Within sixteen years 60 out of 100 would have died. Twenty-six years later 75 would have died. Within forty-six years 90 would have died and only 3 out of the 100 would have reached age sixty.

Under these circumstances death was everywhere and the resultant anxiety must have been overwhelming. Today, however, death is not such an ever-present dark cloud over every person's life.

Paul's central message addressed every person's existential anxiety concerning death. Thus Paul spoke to one of the central anxieties which confronts every human being, and in pre-industrial society this anxiety must have been overwhelming.

One of the most revealing passages in all of Paul's letters is the following passage from Romans.

> While we were living in the flesh, our sinful passions, aroused by the law, were at work in our members to bear fruit for death. But now we are discharged from the law, dead to that which held us captive, so that we serve not under the old written code but in the new life of the Spirit. (*Rom.* 7: 5)

This passage might mean that when Paul was a believer and enforcer of Mosaic law, as was desired by the High Priest, it led him to be a murderer in the name of the law of Moses which was considered to have been given to Moses by God. Through his conversion disorder, however, he was liberated from being held captive to the law, and as a result of this change, he looked inwardly where he found a new way of living by following the indwelling spirit of God.

The question of what will allay a person's existential anxiety concerning death is very important, as we have seen. In the case of Paul his belief in the 'resurrected' Jesus Christ allayed this anxiety. This is the religious dimension of Paul's immortality system and since it is a belief that has a naturalistic explanation, as it arose from what I have argued was the mystical dimension of an episode of conversion disorder, it cannot be used as evidence for the actual physical resurrection of Jesus of Nazareth.

The power of this belief is very clear in the writings of the much respected author Tom Harpur in his book *For Christ's Sake*. Most of Harpur's book is an excellent presentation of all the arguments for the humanity of Jesus of Nazareth. But at the end of his book he affirms that Jesus Christ was raised from the dead by God. The immortality system devised by Paul still operates in Harpur's own faith system. The following quote will show how powerful this immortality system remains to this very day. Tom Harpur wrote:

> The faith that Jesus, who was crucified, who died and was buried, was later seen alive by the Apostles and large groups of the disciples is the foundation of Christian life and belief. Nobody with the slightest

knowledge of the New Testament documents can fail to see this faith as the very heartbeat of the earliest Church, and so it has continued down the ages. As St Paul says, if Christ was not raised from the dead, we are the most miserable of all people. (*1 Cor.* 15: 13-19)

I feel wholly at one with that tradition. In studying the New Testament and the history of the early Church, I have examined this Easter faith from every possible angle. That Jesus was given victory over death, that his steadfast trust in his 'Father' in heaven vindicated, that love was proven stronger than the bonds of mortality, that here we receive a foretaste of a glory prepared for each and every one of us – all this I believe with all my heart and mind. (Harpur, p.80)

It is clear from this quote that Harpur holds a very important belief, and this belief allays his existential anxiety concerning his own death. This belief, however, originated in Paul's experience of what he believed was unification with the resurrected Jesus Christ. This unification experience came out of his conversion disorder. Since the question of what will allay a person's anxiety concerning death is an individual matter there can be no quarrel with Harpur's faith, providing he doesn't attempt to force his belief on others and allows freedom of belief in religious matters. The fact is, however, that Paul's system of allaying a person's existential anxiety concerning the idea of one's death is not the only system. Indeed, every great religion addresses this same problem and the answers in the great religions are quite different from one another. Becker wrote:

All historical religions addressed themselves to this same problem of how to bear the end of life. (Becker, p.12)

Harpur's faith, as with that of all others, no matter how deeply believed, cannot be used as an argument for the 'resurrection' of Jesus, but only as a belief which functions to allay one's personal existential anxiety concerning death.

Paul's Dynamic Faith

We can extract from Paul's writings a value structure which might have universal appeal in our own time. We need a religious point of view which is as universal and inclusive as possible. Paul argued that every human being should have a good internal system of values. If these values are central in a person's life then the enforcement of law becomes unnecessary.

All who have sinned without the law will also perish without the law, and all who have sinned under the law will be judged by the law. *For*

99

it is not the hearers of the law who are righteous before God, but the doers of the law who will be justified. When Gentiles who have not the law do by nature what the law requires, they are a law to themselves, even though they do not have the law. *They show that what the law requires is written on their hearts...* (*Rom.* 2: 12-15, my italics).

Paul was certainly familiar with and relied upon the prophetic literature of the Jewish scriptures. At the end of the book of Romans Paul wrote that we are strengthened by 'the revelation of the mystery which was kept secret for long ages but is now disclosed, and through the prophetic writings is made known to all nations...' (*Rom.* 16: 25-26) The internal writing of the law upon the hearts of people is very clear in Jeremiah:

But this is the covenant which I will make with the house of Israel after those days, says the Lord: I will put my law within them, and *I will write it upon their hearts*; and I will be their God, and they shall be my people. (*Jer.* 31: 33, my italics)

In Romans, Paul writes with the greatest clarity about the importance of love as it relates to the law of Moses:

Owe no one anything, except to love one another; for he who loves his neighbour has fulfilled the law. The commandments, 'You shall not commit adultery, You shall not kill, You shall not steal, You shall not covet', and any other commandment, are summed up in this sentence, 'You shall love your neighbour as yourself.' Love does no wrong to a neighbour; therefore love is the fulfilling of the law. (*Rom.* 13: 8-10)

Here Paul has drawn on *Leviticus* 19: 18 which states 'You shall not take vengeance or bear any grudge against the sons of your own people, but you shall love your neighbour as yourself: I am the Lord.'

Since Paul's background was both Greek and Hebrew he was forced to rethink the meaning of Mosaic law. Paul did not reject the Torah but he observed that those who were supposed to be under the law have also violated the law. He also saw that some who were not under the law lived according to the law. Thus he advocated that good values should be internalized. In this case he used circumcision as an example.

Circumcision indeed is of value if you obey the law; but if you break the law, your circumcision becomes uncircumcision. So, if a man who is uncircumcised keeps the precepts of the law, will not his uncircumcision be regarded as circumcision? Then those who are physically uncircumcised but keep the law will condemn you who have the written code and circumcision but break the law. For he is not a real Jew who is one outwardly, nor is true circumcision something external and physical. *He is a Jew who is one inwardly, and real circumcision is a matter of the heart, spiritual and not literal.* His praise is not from men but from God. (*Rom.* 2: 25-29, my italics)

Throughout Paul's letters he has either drawn on Jewish scriptures or he reflects their point of view in many of his ideas. On the issue of circumcision this precise point of view is found in the prophet Jeremiah.

Behold, the days are coming, says the Lord, when I will punish all those *who are circumcised but yet uncircumcised* – Egypt, Judah, Edom, the sons of Ammon, Moab, and all who dwell in the desert that cut the corners of their hair; for all these nations are uncircumcised, and *all the house of Israel is uncircumcised.* (*Jeremiah* 9: 25-26, my italics)

Paul's concept of living by the Spirit included living by a set of values that has been internalized. Paul's concept of internalization is expressed by writing that 'if we live by the Spirit, let us also walk by the Spirit.' A person will never come into conflict with the law if that person lives by the Spirit. This was the ultimate step which Paul took in his liberation from the law of Moses although he never rejected the law. Paul's concept of justification by faith alone implied the internalization of a set of values which, if followed, would result in good works which could not, therefore, be in conflict with the law. The following quote from Paul shows the turning-point in his value system.

But I say, walk by the Spirit and do not gratify the desires of the flesh... But *if you are led by the Spirit you are not under the law. Now the works of the flesh* are plain: immorality, impurity, licentiousness, idolatry, sorcery, enmity, strife, jealousy, anger, selfishness, dissension, party spirit, envy, drunkenness, carousing, and the like... But *the fruit of the Spirit is love, joy, peace, patience, kindness, goodness, faithfulness, gentleness, self-control; against such there is no law...* If we live by the Spirit, let us also walk by the Spirit. Let us have no self-conceit, no provoking of one another, no envy of one another. (*Gal.* 5: 16, 18-23, 25-26, my italics)

Paul took one further step in his effort to liberate himself from the law of Moses. Paul argued that Abraham predated Moses and Abraham did not have the law. Abraham went forth out of Ur of the Chaldees on a promise from God. Abraham went forth on the basis of faith. Therefore, faith takes precedence over the law of Moses. Paul wrote:

> This is what I mean: the law, which came four hundred and thirty years afterward [after Abraham], does not annul a covenant previously ratified by God, so as to make the promise void. For if the inheritance is by the law, it is no longer by promise; but God gave it to Abraham by a promise. (*Gal.* 3: 17-18)

Paul then argues that when Christ came, faith was restored:

> Now before faith came, we were confined under the law, kept under restraint until faith should be revealed, so that the law was our custodian until Christ came, that we might be justified by faith. But now that faith has come, we are no longer under a custodian; for in Christ Jesus you are all sons of God through faith... There is neither Jew nor Greek, there is neither slave nor free, there is neither male nor female; for you are all one in Christ Jesus. (*Gal.* 3: 23-28)

Paul argues that if you are in the Spirit then the greatest spiritual gift of all is love. This led Paul to write his enduring hymn to love. He wrote:

> If I speak in the tongues of men and of angels, but have not love, I am a noisy gong or a clanging cymbal. And if I have prophetic powers, and understand all mysteries and all knowledge, and if I have all faith, so as to remove mountains, but have not love, I am nothing. If I give away all I have, and if I deliver my body to be burned, but have not love, I am nothing.
>
> Love is patient and is kind; love is not jealous or boastful... Love does not insist on its own way; it is not irritable or resentful; it does not rejoice at wrong, but rejoices in the right. Love bears all things, believes all things, hopes all things, endures all things.
>
> Love never ends; as for prophecy, it will pass away; as for tongues, they will cease; as for knowledge, it will pass away. For our knowledge is imperfect and our prophecy is imperfect; but when the perfect comes, the imperfect will pass away. When I was a child, I spoke like a child... I reasoned like a child; when I became a man, I gave up childish ways. For now we see in a mirror dimly, but then face to face. Now I know in part; then I shall understand fully, even as I have been fully understood. So faith, hope, love abide, these three: but the greatest of these is love. (*1 Cor.* 13: 1-13)

Near the end of Philippians Paul wrote a brief summary of his point of view:

> Finally, brethren, whatever is true, whatever is honourable, whatever is just, whatever is pure, whatever is lovely, whatever is gracious; if

there be any virtue, if there is anything worthy of praise, think about these things. (*Phil.* 4: 8)

Paul thought that his religious insights were universal and applied to every human being.

... And let us not grow weary in well-doing, for in due season we shall reap, if we do not lose heart. So then, as we have opportunity, let us do good to all men. (*Gal.* 6: 9-10)

The Little Sermon on the Mount

Paul did not give emphasis to the religion taught by the historical Jesus, since he claimed that his religion came directly from the 'resurrected' Jesus Christ. Yet the influence of James and Peter must have made a small impact upon Paul because in *Romans* 12: 9-21 Paul wrote a summary of his version of the SERMON ON THE MOUNT (Wolfe, p.373). It is useful to review Paul's version of the religion of Jesus. Paul wrote:

Let love be genuine; hate what is evil, hold fast to what is good; love one another with brotherly affection; outdo one another in showing honour. Never flag in zeal, be aglow with the Spirit, serve the Lord. Rejoice in your hope, be patient in tribulation, be constant in prayer. Contribute to the needs of the saints, practice hospitality.

Bless those who persecute you; bless and do not curse them. Rejoice with those who rejoice, weep with those who weep. Live in harmony with one another; do not be haughty, but associate with the lowly; never be conceited. Repay no one evil for evil, but take thought for what is noble in the sight of all. If possible, so far as it depends upon you, live peaceably with all. Beloved, never avenge yourselves, but leave it to the wrath of God; for it is written, 'Vengeance is mine, I will repay, says the Lord.' No, 'if your enemy is hungry, feed him; if he is thirsty, give him drink; for by so doing you will make him feel ashamed of himself for what he has done to you.' Do not try to overcome evil with evil, but overcome evil with good. (The last part of the above quote is taken from the *Living Bible.*)

Paul has been a towering figure in the history of Christianity and he has been much misunderstood because his religious system emerged from a deep psychological trauma on the road to Damascus. Today, we know that Paul never knew what actually happened to him since conversion disorder and its accompanying feelings of unification with a higher power are involuntary and result from an unresolved unconscious conflict. Yet, that experience turned Paul from the strict enforcement of the externals of the law to the deep insight that what really counts in any person's life is a good system of internalized values. Paul also knew that it was not enough to espouse values and not follow those values in daily living. The very best summary of Paul's religion is contained in this line from his writings:

If we live by the Spirit, let us also walk by the Spirit. (*Gal.* 5: 25)

Chapter 8

The Human Response to Death

The Christian myth of the Resurrection, the Ascension, and the Pentecost has been woven into the religious life of the Western World. This myth, when approached from the point of view of grief rather than resurrection, yields a different set of meanings from our traditional Christian heritage. What is important is not what happened historically, but the development of faith. Whatever may have happened historically is not as important as the emergence of a myth which addressed the human anxiety that surrounds death. All authorities agree that Jesus died on a cross. Out of Jesus' death emerge two concerns: 1) As Jesus had to face the idea of his own death, every thinking person should, at sometime in his or her life, confront the reality that they, too, will die; and 2) just as Mary Magdalene and the disciples had to struggle with the death of Jesus, every person must at sometime, in his or her life, struggle with the death of loved ones or close friends.

What is the nature of a faith that sustains a person for creative living while facing their own death or the death of other people? These issues are addressed by a step of faith and by a deep and abiding appreciation of life.

Therefore, in what follows I will discuss two issues. What is the nature of a faith that will allay the anxiety that surrounds the idea of my own death? What is the nature of our faith when we confront the death of loved ones and close friends?

Confronting the Existential Anxiety Surrounding One's Own Death

Ernest Becker, in his book *The Denial of Death*, has given an excellent summary of contemporary psychoanalytical thinking on the meaning of death. In the preface to his book he wrote:

The prospect of death, Dr Johnson said, wonderfully concentrates the mind. The main thesis of this book is that it does much more than that: the idea of death, the fear of it, haunts the human animal like nothing else; it is the mainspring of human activity designed largely to avoid the fatality of death, to overcome it by denying in some way that it is the final destiny for man. The fear of death is indeed a universal in the human condition. (Becker, ix)

In contemporary society death is a subject which is avoided. Few people are comfortable with a serious consideration of the idea of their own death, and the resulting fear of death gives rise to a largely unconscious anxiety. Becker, through his summary of Kierkegaard, identifies the anxiety surrounding death which confronts every fully aware human being. This anxiety is the utter reality that, in the end, every person dies. This is the truth that most people will not discuss or face as being their own destiny. Becker wrote:

The foundation stone for Kierkegaard's view of man is... the basic insight of psychology for all time: that man is a union of opposites, of self-consciousness and of a physical body. Man emerged from the instinctive thoughtless action of the lower animals and came to reflect on his condition. He was given a consciousness of his individuality and his part-divinity in creation, the beauty and uniqueness of his face and his name. At the same time he was given the consciousness of the terror of the world and of his own death and decay. *This paradox is the really constant thing about man in all periods of history and society; it is thus the true essence of man...* The fall into self-consciousness, the emergence from comfortable ignorance in nature, had one great penalty for man: it gave him dread or anxiety... Man's anxiety is a function of his sheer ambiguity and of his complete powerlesness to overcome ambiguity, to be straightforwardly an animal or an angel. He cannot live heedless of his fate, nor can he take sure control over that fate and triumph over it by being outside the human condition. (Becker, pp.68-69, my italics)

The myth of the death and resurrection of Jesus of Nazareth led Christian theologians to hammer out a subsequent myth – the myth of the doctrine of the Holy Trinity. This myth is very important because it confirms, in theological terms, the eternal dilemma of humankind's existential situation.

The doctrine of the Holy Trinity asserts that God is one but God is manifested in three aspects. These aspects are God the Father, God the Son, and God the Holy Spirit. I propose that in the myth of the Holy Trinity, God the Father symbolizes the creative powers in the universe, God the Son relates to humankind which was brought into being by the creative powers, and God the Holy Spirit gives emphasis to the creative power which is in every human being.

The historical doctrine of the Trinity affirms as a dogma that God the Son, or Jesus Christ, has two natures. He was 100% God and at the same time he was 100% human. That is, Jesus Christ was God in his total nature but he was also subject to death because he was 100% human.

I am arguing that the existential reality of the two sides of every human being was projected onto Jesus Christ, the second person of the Trinity, and these two dimensions of the human being should confront every aware person. On the one hand, we are like God in our ability to contemplate infinity; that is, symbolically we are out of nature. But on the other hand, we are also human beings subject to the reality of death. This basic contradiction in humankind's essential nature, as reflected in the second person of the Trinity, was declared a holy mystery by the Christian church. This reality of the human situation was expressed theologically, but it contained the essential insight now confirmed by the observations of contemporary psychologists that every human being has two natures – one symbolically out of nature and the other is like an animal that dies. This is the reality of humankind's existence and this awareness produces anxiety.

Ernest Becker does not make the connection between the myth of the two natures of Jesus Christ as contained in the second person in the Holy Trinity and the essential psychological insight into the nature of people, but in the following quote from him the connection can be readily inferred. Becker quotes Erich Fromm as follows:

> ... the essence of man is really his PARADOXICAL nature, the fact that he is half animal and half symbolic... We might call this existential paradox the condition of INDIVIDUALITY WITHIN FINITUDE. Man has a symbolic identity that brings him sharply out of nature. He is a symbolic self, a creature with a name, a life history. He is a creator with a mind that soars up to speculate about atoms and infinity, who can place himself imaginatively at a point in space and contemplate bemusedly his own planet. This immense expansion, this dexterity, this ethereality, this self-consciousness gives to man literally the status of a small god in nature, as Renaissance thinkers knew.
>
> Yet, at the same time, as the Eastern sages also knew, man is a worm and food for worms. This is the paradox: he is out of nature and hopelessly in it; he is dual, up in the stars and yet housed in a heart-

pumping, breath-gasping body that once belonged to a fish and still carries the gill marks to prove it. His body is a material flesh casing that is alien to him in many ways – the strangest and most repugnant way being that it aches and bleeds and will decay and die. Man is literally split in two: he has an awareness of his own splendid uniqueness in that he sticks out of nature with a towering majesty, and yet he goes back into the ground a few feet in order blindly and dumbly to rot and disappear forever. It is a terrifying dilemma to be in and to have to live with... everything that man does in his symbolic world is an attempt to deny and overcome his grotesque fate. (Becker, pp.26-27)

The idea that anxiety confronts every aware human being, as suggested by Becker, Kierkegaard, and Fromm, is found in Tom Robbins' popular book *Jitterbug Perfume*. Robbins wrote:

If a person leads an 'active' life, as Wiggs had, if a person has goals, ideals, a cause to fight for, then that person is distracted, temporarily, from paying a whole lot of attention to the heavy scimitar that hangs by a mouse hair just above his or her head. We, each of us, have a ticket to ride, and if the trip be interesting (if it's dull, we have only ourselves to blame), then we relish the landscape (how quickly it whizzes by!), interact with our fellow travellers, pay frequent visits to the washrooms and concession stands, and hardly ever hold up the ticket to the light where we can read its plainly stated destination: The Abyss.

Yet, ignore it though we might in our daily toss and tussle, the fact of our impending death is always there, just behind the draperies, or, more accurately, inside our sock, like a burr that we can never quite extract... Ah, but the spectre is there, night and day, day in and day out, colouring with its chalk of gray almost everything we do. And a lot of what we do is done, subconsciously, indirectly, to avoid the thought of death, or to make ourselves so unexpendable through our accomplishments that death will hesitate to take us, or, when the scimitar finally falls, to insure that we will 'live on' in the memory of the lucky ones still kicking. (Robbins, p.281)

If the psychological view of the essential nature of people is correct, then every person, either consciously or unconsciously, fashions some kind of faith which is designed to allay the dread which surrounds death.

The great issues of life are really understood when they are experienced in a personal way. This fundamental insight gave rise to the existentialist philosophical movement, which ranked thinking about our existence as being higher than speculative or scientific thought. Ian Henderson, who was Professor of Systematic Theology at the University of Glasgow in Scotland, wrote:

> Kierkegaard, whose thinking was bound up with his own inwardly troubled life, broke away from the tradition of Western philosophy by ranking speculative thinking lower than existential. The latter is the kind of thinking we carry on when we are making up our mind whether to marry a particular person, or whether we ought to emigrate, or when we are working out our proper vocation in life, or when we are facing the imminent prospect of death. Utterly removed from the dispassionate, spectator-like attitude of the normal philosopher or scientist, it is characterized by decision, isolation, and an absence of demonstrative certainty. Kierkegaard insisted that this, and not abstract reasoning, was the highest type of mental activity for us... (Loetscher, p.409)

I want to share the following personal experiences because they are existential in nature. The existential anxiety which surrounds death has been a part of my own life over the last eighteen years. In 1981 I suffered a major heart attack and, after excellent medical advice from a highly competent cardiologist and an outstanding surgeon, I checked into the hospital where I had a four-way bypass operation. The operation was successful and after a short period of recovery I was back at my usual activities. In this first surgery the deep awareness of the possibility of death was not foremost in my thinking. The thought of death was pushed aside by my basic confidence that I would go through the surgery with no complications.

In 1986, however, I had another heart attack which required a second heart operation. I had great faith in the medical team that would do the surgery and their support staff, but this time death was foremost in my mind.

In the middle of the night before my second surgery I was deeply aware that I might die on the operating table. My chances of surviving were good but no person can determine, in advance, whether he will or will not be among those who do not survive the operation. I was aware of the deep anxiety which I had concerning my own death. It was at this moment that I confronted my existential anxiety and went through the following steps. I accepted the fact that I might be dead in a few hours but I also said to myself, 'When I go under the anaesthetic my conscious mind will be blocked out; therefore, I place my total being in the care of my unconscious mind or in the life force which is within me. I now surrender my self to the elemental forces embedded in life.' In addition I said the following to my unconscious

109

mind, 'I trust you. I thank you for having pulled me through this once before. You know what this is going to be like so I place my faith in your strength and wisdom. I have faith in you to keep me alive.'

When I absorbed these feelings of trust into my own being I knew that I had confronted the possibility of my own death and its resultant anxiety. Through an act of faith in the strength of life I had allayed my anxiety by absorbing it into a very strong faith, and as a result resurrected my own courage and strength and was able to face my own surgery and the possibility of death.

When this became clear in my mind and feelings, I was reminded of the 23rd Psalm in which the existential anxiety surrounding death had been faced by the author of the Psalm. The King James Version is as follows:

> Yea, though I walk through the valley of the shadow of death, I will fear no evil for thou art with me.

In my mind I changed the verse as follows:

> Yea, though I walk through the valley of the shadow of death, I will have no anxiety, no matter what I have to face, because the creative power of life is within me and will sustain me.

The myth of the death and resurrection of Jesus Christ is a mirror of the deep psychological reality that every person faces when death is confronted and the resultant anxiety is converted into faith. In a sense every person faces small 'deaths' and 'resurrections' as they go through life. That is, a small part of oneself must 'die' in order for a new part to live. In a sense this is a 'death' and a 'resurrection'. This is one religious dimension of the myth of the death and resurrection of Jesus Christ.

However, there is no universally accepted faith formula which will allay every person's existential anxiety. Every person must find his or her own response to the dread of death, but that very necessary response must come out of the ideology, the awareness, the value core, and the belief or faith structure of each individual.

The last line in Becker's book is excellent:

> The most that anyone of us can seem to do is to fashion something – an object or ourselves – and drop it into the confusion (of living), (and) make an offering of it, so to speak, to the life force. (Becker, p285)

The Social Response to the Death of a Loved One

When we mourn the loss of a loved one or a friend we become

involved in culturally-defined acts which are performed at the time of death and for a time after death.

The function of mourning customs are to assist the living to cope emotionally with their loss, to assist the living to work through their grief, and to assist the living to reintegrate into society. Emotional healing and reintegration require a reasonable correspondence between the culturally-defined mourning acts and the time required for healing to occur.

In contemporary society the wider social response to the death of a loved one centres around the funeral service; therefore, I want to review Arnold van Gennep's classical work on rites of passage in funerals, and then mention some aspects of contemporary mourning.

In Arnold van Gennep's classic book *Rites of Passage*, published in 1908, he provided anthropologists with the concepts of separation, transition, and incorporation. The basic data that he used in the development of his ideas was drawn from studies done in the early nineteenth century of 'primitive' societies.

At the beginning of van Gennep's chapter on FUNERALS he wrote:

> On first considering funeral ceremonies, one expects rites of separation to be their most prominent component, in contrast to rites of incorporation, which should be only slightly elaborated. A study of the data, however, reveals that the rites of separation are few in number and very simple, while the transition rites have a duration and complexity sometimes so great that they must be granted a sort of autonomy. Furthermore, those funeral rites which incorporate the deceased into the world of the dead are most extensively elaborated and assigned the greatest importance. (van Gennep, p.146)

The funeral rites in primitive cultures make no sense unless they are seen against the background of their firm faith in an afterlife.

All of the rites in 'primitive' societies which were described by van Gennep depend upon a concept of a world or worlds beyond the grave to which the deceased travel following death. Van Gennep outlines the most generally held idea of the afterlife. He wrote:

> The most widespread idea is that of a world analogous to ours, but more pleasant, and of a society organized in the same way as it is here. Thus everyone re-enters again the categories of clan, age group, or occupation that he had on earth... The journey to the other world and the entrance to it comprise a series of rites of passage whose details depend on the distance and topography of that world. (van Gennep, pp.152-153)

111

Concerning mourning, van Gennep wrote:

Mourning is a transitional period for the survivors; they enter it through rites of separation and emerge from it through rites of reintegration into society (rites of the lifting of mourning). In some cases, the transitional period of the living is a counterpart of the transitional period of the deceased, and the termination of the first sometimes coincides with the termination of the second – that is, with the incorporation of the deceased into the world of the dead. (van Gennep, p.147)

In order to understand the rites of separation, transition and incorporation the following examples are taken from van Gennep's book, although Van Gennep gives no examples of separation rites. Separation was virtually ignored in the mourning rites.

The next phase in rites of passage is the transitional period in funeral rites. Van Gennep wrote:

The transitional period in funeral rites is first marked physically by the more or less extended stay of the corpse or the coffin in the deceased's room (as during a wake), in the vestibule of his house, or elsewhere. (van Gennep, p.148)

The incorporation rites which were designed to integrate the dead into the afterlife were extensive. There is not always a sharp distinction between transition and incorporation. In the case of a Toda man, van Gennep wrote:

He is taken to the burial place of his clan and deposited in the boat on the frozen ground, with his feet facing north, surrounded with all the things he will need in the next world. The deceased is thought to partake of a farewell meal eaten on the spot by the mourners, who then all leave... The dead go by a long and tortuous route toward the north, where the dark and cold land of the dead is located... Thus there is a series of preliminary rites, a transitional period, and a final funeral when the dead person reaches his final abode. (van Gennep, p.38)

Mourning customs vary from one group to another, and they vary from individual to individual depending upon the closeness of the individual to the deceased.

It should be clear that in funerals the most extensive rites in the book *Rites of Passage* are those that deal with transition and incorporation, because the societies that were studied held very clear ideas about the afterlife. In order for the deceased to enter the afterlife elaborate and time-consuming rites were required. Sometimes the rites would require as much time as two and a half years.

This much attention has been devoted to van Gennep's ideas of rites and mourning, because in 'primitive' societies belief in an after-life demanded that the deceased be properly incorporated into that world. In fact, however, what probably happened was that by the time the rites were concluded the survivors were over their grief and re-integrated into their own society. Thus there was a correspondence between the actual rite structure and the time required for the living to be reintegrated into their own social structure.

In contemporary Christian society the normal and customary funer-al rites are extremely short and there is no possibility that our rites could extend over a two to three year period as in primitive societies. However, our present custom of holding a funeral service a few days after the death of the deceased, with the family and friends gather-ing for a brief period of mourning and then returning to their normal daily activities, hardly meets the minimum time required for healthy mourning. Contemporary mourning customs in North America almost ignore the bereaved's need for transition and reintegration into their own society.

The Hope of a More Intelligent Response to Death and Bereavement

Quite frequently, those who survive the death of a loved one do not have a supportive network which can help them make all of the necessary changes required in bereavement. It is true that most people will have friends and in many, many cases there will be some mem-bers of the family who will rally around and give some assistance to those in bereavement. In earlier societies, which were much more intimate, there was always someone in the community who knew what was happening to every person in the village or at the farm. Under these conditions a networking system was in effect and arose out of normal interpersonal relationships.

When I was a minister in a small town in New England, many years ago, I received a telephone call one morning advising me that I should call on Mrs Johnson, because the first thing that she does in the morn-ing is to roll up the blind and when she does not roll up her blind she is usually sick. She had not rolled up her blind. I called on her in the late morning and she was indeed ill. I was then able to set in motion all necessary medical help and community support. This easy and informal system has been lost in most communities in today's society.

113

In order to fill this void there have been several organizations which are responding with a deep caring motive.

In 1975 Dr Kenneth Haugk, a minister and clinical psychologist, began the concept of THE STEPHENS MINISTRY. This movement has taken root in over 2,200 churches and in 53 denominations world wide. It was designed to expand 'the quality and quantity of Christian care that a congregation can provide its members by equipping lay persons to make weekly, one-on-one visits to individuals needing Christian care and support' (Haugk, *The Stephens Series* 1).

The Stephens Series equips lay people to provide an effective caring ministry in many categories of human need, including the terminally ill and the bereaved. Those lay people who are trained in this ministry volunteer their time and respond to those who need help following the death of a loved one. Here is the beginning of a well-thought-out social response to those who are experiencing grief.

The problem with the Stephens Ministry is that it is church based and, since only 30% of the population in the United States is churched and even fewer are churched in Canadian society, this leaves a vast majority of the population without the benefit of this well-thought-out network.

Another organization that is trying to respond to the needs of those experiencing grief is the HOSPICE SOCIETY. Their members are well organized and well trained, and the organization is non-denominational; thus, they respect the diverse customs and cultural traditions in death and dying. Each member of the Hospice Society is trained to respond to any person's grief with quiet assistance, encouragement and caring.

They have trained volunteers who provide support and information to people who are dying, grieving or involved with someone who is confronting the loss of a loved one. In addition, they have a community out-reach program which offers speakers for groups and workshops, and they have a lending library of books, tapes, and videos. This again is a social response to the concerns which must be faced when the living confront the loss of someone who was deeply loved.

In addition to these organizations there are counselling services which are readily available to any individual who realizes that bereavement can have serious consequences in any person's life and that sometimes it is useful to seek the benefit of contemporary knowledge about grief and grieving.

Van Gennep wrote at the turn of this century. Since that time there have been many studies of grief and mourning, and there is beginning to be a much greater understanding of the emotional needs of those who have suffered the loss of a mate or a close friend.

Conclusion

In this book I have argued that when the Christian myths are approached from a modern psychological point of view they yield a set of meanings which are very important to the understanding of the emergence of Christianity and they still point to very important areas of human experience.

I have argued that Mary Magdalene and the disciples believed that Jesus was 'resurrected' because they experienced grief-related hallucinations of Jesus of Nazareth. Also, I have argued that the myth of the Resurrection, the Ascension, and the Pentecost is an externalized bereavement process. Thus, this myth gives emphasis to the importance of grief in human society.

I have also argued that the apostle Paul suffered conversion disorder on the road to Damascus and that out of the mystical component of this psychological trauma he passionately believed that Jesus had been resurrected from the dead by a unilateral act of God. Paul also believed that if any person accepted Jesus Christ as Lord, that person would also be resurrected from the dead and have eternal life. From my perspective Paul's belief was a myth because Jesus was never resurrected from the dead. Paul, however, changed from the enforcement of the law to a good internal set of values, and belief in the myth addressed every believer's existential anxiety concerning death. These, too, are eternal human concerns.

Above all, every thinking human being is forced to confront the existential anxiety which comes from the awareness that all flesh is mortal. In the face of such anxiety, each person develops a faith of some kind which addresses and allays the anxiety which surrounds the idea of one's own death.

I like the following quotation:

To laugh often and love much; to win and hold the respect of intelligent persons and the affection of little children; to earn the approbation of honest critics and to endure without flinching the betrayal of false friends; to appreciate beauty always, whether in earth's creations or man's handiwork; to have sought for and found the best in others, and to have given it oneself; to leave the world better than one found it, whether by a healthy child, a garden patch, a cheery letter, or a redeemed social condition; to have played with enthusiasm, laughed with exuberance, and sung with exaltation; to go down to dust and dreams knowing that the world is a wee bit better, and that even a single life breathes easier because we have lived well – this is to have succeeded.

Author unknown

END NOTES

1. When I began writing this book I could not find a single scholar who was writing along the same train of thought as me. Since that time, I am happy to say that John Dominic Crossan has been courageous enough to tackle the psychological problems which were faced by Mary Magdalene, the disciples and the apostle Paul.

John Dominic Crossan, in his book *Jesus: A Revolutionary Biography*, wrote that Paul fell into a trance and while in a trance he had a revelatory experience of Christ, and this experience was dissociative in nature. In psychiatry, dissociative is defined as a mental disorder in which there is a sudden temporary alteration in consciousness, identity, or motor behaviour. From my point of view, Crossan is correct; however, he does not give any analysis of what might have led Paul to have had a dissociative experience.

Also, Crossan dismisses the experiences of Mary Magdalene and the disciples because they did not fall into a trance. Crossan has failed to make a distincion between the illusions which are grief-related and those which come from conversion disorder.

This is important because Crossan is attempting to give a psychological analysis of the founding events in the Christian church. Indeed, this is a refreshing scholarly attempt to use modern knowledge to understand what might have happened in the Christian church. In his latest book, *The Birth of Christianity* (1998), Crossan brings an interesting passage:

> Not only were visions and apparitions an accepted and even commonplace possibility in the early first century, they are also an accepted and even commonplace possibility in the late twentieth. In a paper presented to the Spring 1995 meeting of the Jesus Seminar, Stacy Davids summarized recent psychiatric literature on grief and bereavement: 'A review of well-conducted studies of the past three decades shows that about 50% to 80% of bereaved people studied feel this intuitive, sometimes overwhelming *presence* or *spirit* of the lost person... These perceptions happen most often in the first few months following the death, but sometimes persist more than a year, with significantly more women than men reporting these events... The American Psychiatric Association, author of *The Diagnostic and Statistical Manual of Mental Disorders* – IV, considers the phenomena (when 'one hears the voice of, or transiently sees the image of, the deceased person') as non-pathological. (pp.XVI-XVII)

It is, however, true that Crossan and I differ on several points.

119

2. There has always been considerable debate as to whether Jesus' body was placed in a tomb. The Anglican Bishop Barnes, Bishop of Birmingham, wrote:

> After the crufixion of Jesus they (the followers of Jesus) were scattered fugitives, followers of a man who came to a criminal's end, whose body quite possibly had been flung ignominiously into a common malefactor's grave. (Barnes, p.174)

See also p.88.

3. The *Oxford Annotated Bible: Revised Standard Version* uses the word 'appearance' where the King James Version of the New Testament uses the word 'seen'.

4. The idea that Mary Magdalene and the disciples saw hallucinations of Jesus of Nazareth is an old idea, and it has been essentially rejected by previous scholars. The argument for rejecting the hallucinatory theory rested on the assumption that only one person could see an hallucination of the deceased at any given time. Furthermore, there was only one type of hallucination which was considered.

According to contemporary scholars it is now well known that there are at least five types of hallucinations or illusions. It is possible that one person may have one type of illusion and another person have a different illusion. It is possible that several people can have the same illusion at the same time. Grief-related hallucinations and illusions are widely accepted in psychiatric circles and they are considered to be quite normal accompaniments of grief.

5. This is not her real name.

6. This is not his real name.

7. I am indebted to Dr Robert Kimball for having discussed these ideas with me. He has been of great help to me at every turn in the writing of this manuscript.

8. In the book of Acts the actual quote is 'Saul, Saul why do you persecute me?' I have not used the name Saul because I think this carries anti-Jewish overtones. When Paul was carrying out his persecutions he was Jewish, and when he changed his religious outlook and developed his own religion he was known as Paul. I use the name Paul because he was the same person all the time.

9. Dr Raymond Archer, retired professor of philosophy, University of Regina, in a personal letter to me, dated 25 February 1994.

10. As we proceed, it will become quite clear that Paul thought God had resurrected Jesus from the dead but Jesus was not God. Paul was always quite clear about distinguishing between God and Jesus. I have called this

point of view Pauline Christianity in order to separate it from the type of Trinitarian Christianity which, much later, made Jesus into a God who was 100% human and 100% God.

11. This is speculation on my part. There is no way of knowing what actually happened between Ananias and Paul. We do know that his conflict, whatever it might have been, was resolved, and he regained his sight.

12. There is no way of confirming whether this experience took place on the road to Damascus or not. It is interesting that Paul writes of this traumatic experience yet the timing is not in accordance with some authorities. I have assumed that this was the turning-point in his life, but I cannot confirm this with any certainty.

13. This is very important because it distinguishes Paul from what later became Christianity.

14. Dr Gary R Habermas is a professor at Liberty University and Director of Liberty's Master's program in Apologetics. He holds a PhD from Michigan State University and he has written four books on the subject of the resurrection. He is a specialist on the historical evidence which can be used to sustain the belief that the resurrection actually occurred.

15. Dr Antony G N Flew was for many years professor of philosophy at the University of Reading, England. He has taught at Christ Church, University of Oxford, and at many universities around the world. He holds the MA from St John's College, University of Oxford, and a D LITT from the University of Keele. He is the author of sixteen books and numerous articles, and in this debate represented the atheistic point of view.

16. This debate, held on 2 May 1985 and attended by more than 3000 people, was of great significance since the debaters gave the most sophisticated arguments which exist in contemporary philosophy, theology, and historical research, both for and against the resurrection.

Bibliography

American Psychiatric Association, DIAGNOSTIC AND STATISTICAL MANUAL OF MENTAL DISORDERS, Fourth Edition, 1994. (See also Spitzer, Robert L.)

Barnes, Ernest William, THE RISE OF CHRISTIANITY, Longmans, Green & Co., London, New York, Toronto, 1948.

Becker, Ernest, THE DENIAL OF DEATH, The Free Press, New York, 1973.

Breech, James, THE SILENCE OF JESUS, Fortress Press, Philadelphia, 1983.

Campbell, Joseph, MYTHS TO LIVE BY, Bantam Books, New York, 1972.

Carpenter, Joseph Estlin, THE RELATION OF JESUS TO HIS AGE AND OUR OWN ('The Essex Hall Lecture' 1895, London).

Cox, Harvey, THE SILENCING OF LEONARDO BOFF, Meyer Stone Books, Oak Park IL., 1988.

Cross, F. L. and Livingstone, E. A. (Editors), THE OXFORD DICTIONARY OF THE CHRISTIAN CHURCH, Oxford University Press, 1989.

Crossan, John Dominic, THE BIRTH OF CHRISTIANITY, HarperCollins, 1998; T&T Clark, Edinburgh, 1999.

Ellard, J. et al, NORMAL AND PATHOLOGICAL RESPONSES TO BEREAVEMENT, MSS Information Corporation, New York, 1974.

English and English, A COMPREHENSIVE DICTIONARY OF PSYCHOLOGICAL AND PSYCHOANALYTICAL TERMS, Longmans Green and Co., New York, N.Y., 1958

Ferm, Vergilius, AN ENCYCLOPAEDIA OF RELIGION, The Philosophical Library, New York, New York, 1945.

Feuerbach, Ludwig, THE ESSENCE OF CHRISTIANITY, translated by George Eliot, Harper Torchbooks, Harper and Brothers, New York, N.Y., 1957.

Gaston, Lloyd, PAUL AND THE TORAH, University of British Columbia Press, Vancouver, B.C., 1987.

Gennep, van, Arnold, THE RITES OF PASSAGE, translated by Monika B. Vizedom, The University of Chicago Press, 1960. Introduction by Solan Kimball.

Habermas, Gary and Flew, Antony G. N., DID JESUS RISE FROM THE DEAD?, Harper and Row, San Francisco, 1989.

Harpur, Tom, FOR CHRIST'S SAKE, Oxford University Press, Toronto, 1986.

Harris, William H. and Levy, Judith S., Editors, THE NEW COLUMBIA ENCY-CLOPAEDIA, Columbia University Press, New York, N.Y., 1975

Haugk, Kenneth Dr., THE STEPHEN SERIES, Stephen Ministries, 1325 Boland, St. Louis, Missouri.

Hill, Michael, A SOCIOLOGY OF RELIGION, Heinemann Educational Books, Ltd., London, 1976.

Hospice Society of the Comox Valley, *Hospice Flyer*.

James, William, THE VARIETIES OF RELIGIOUS EXPERIENCE, A Mentor Book, published by The New American Library, New York, N.Y., 1958.

Kenny, Michael G., THE PASSION OF ANSEL BOURNE, Smithsonian Institution Press, Washington D.C., 1986.

Koester, Helmut, INTRODUCTION TO THE NEW TESTAMENT, Walter de Gruyter & Co., Berlin, Germany.

Küng, Hans, ON BEING A CHRISTIAN, Doubleday, New York, N.Y., 1984.

Loetscher, Lefferts A., Editor, TWENTIETH CENTURY ENCYCLOPAEDIA OF RELIGIOUS KNOWLEDGE, Baker Book House, Grand Rapids, Michigan, 1955.

Lunny, William J., THE SOCIOLOGY OF THE RESURRECTION, Heron Publishing, Victoria, Canada, 1989.

Maccoby, Hyam, THE MYTHMAKER: PAUL AND THE INVENTION OF CHRISTIANITY, Harper and Row, New York, 1986.

May, Herbert G. and Metzger, Bruce M., Editors, THE OXFORD ANNOTATED BIBLE: REVISED STANDARD VERSION, Oxford University Press, New York, 1962.

Mayer-Gross, W; Slater, Eliot; Roth, Martin, CLINICAL PSYCHIATRY, Cassell and Company Ltd., London, 1955.

Neil, William, HARPER'S BIBLE COMMENTARY, Harper & Row, New York, N.Y., 1962.

Nollen, John Scholte, THE WAY, THE TRUTH, THE LIFE: THE WORDS OF JESUS, The Beacon Press, Boston, 1948.

O'Toole, Roger, RELIGION: CLASSIC SOCIOLOGICAL APPROACHES, University of Toronto, 1984.

Pagels, Elaine, THE GNOSTIC GOSPELS, Random House, New York, 1979.

Peck, Scott M., THE ROAD LESS TRAVELLED, A Touchstone Book, Simon and Schuster, New York, 1978.

Perrin, Norman, THE RESURRECTION ACCORDING TO MATTHEW, MARK AND LUKE, Fortress Press, Philadelphia, 1977.

:   THE NEW TESTAMENT, Harcourt Brace Jovanovich, New York, 1982.

Rees, Dr W Dewi, THE HALLUCINATIONS OF WIDOWHOOD, British Medical Journal, October 1971.

Riley, Gregory J., RESURRECTION RECONSIDERED, Fortress Press, Minneapolis, 1995.

Robbins, Tom, JITTERBUG PERFUME, Bantam, New York, 1985.

Rosenblatt, Paul C., GRIEF AND MOURNING IN CROSS-CULTURAL PERSPECTIVE, Human Relations Area Files, Inc., 1976.

Ross, Hugh McGregor, THE GOSPEL OF THOMAS, William Sessions Limited, The Ebor Press, York, England, 1987.

Sanders, E. P., JESUS AND JUDAISM, Fortress Press, Philadelphia, 1985.

Schonfield, Dr Hugh J., THOSE INCREDIBLE CHRISTIANS, Bantam Books of Canada, Toronto 1968.

Schweitzer, Albert, THE QUEST OF THE HISTORICAL JESUS, Adam & Charles Black, London, 1948

Shuchter, Stephen R., DIMENSIONS OF GRIEF, Jossey-Bass Publishers, San Francisco, 1986.

Spitzer, Robert L. (Chairperson), DIAGNOSTIC AND STATISTICAL MANUAL OF MENTAL DISORDERS, Third Edition, The American Psychiatric Association, 1980. (See also American Psychiatric Association).

Spong, John Shelby, RESURRECTION MYTH OR REALITY? Harper-SanFrancisco, HarperCollins Publishers, New York, N.Y., 1994

Steiner, Claude M., SCRIPTS PEOPLE LIVE, Bantam Book, Grove Press, New York, New York, 1974.

Stendhal, Kirster, PAUL AMONG JEWS AND GENTILES, Fortress Press, Philadelphia, 1976.

Stimpson, George, A BOOK ABOUT THE BIBLE, Harper and Brothers, New York, 1945.

Tucker, Judi, ORIENTATION TO PALLIATIVE CARE, Algonquin College Printers, Algonquin College, 1986.

Wilbur, Earl Morse, OUR UNITARIAN HERITAGE, The Beacon Press, Boston, 1925.

Wilson, Colin, AFTERLIFE, Doubleday & Company, Inc., Garden City, New York, 1987.

Wolfe, Rolland Emerson, THE TWELVE RELIGIONS OF THE BIBLE, The Edwin Mellen Press, New York and Toronto, 1982.

Index

Some other books published by

OPEN GATE PRESS

incorporating Centaur Press (1954)

*

Frankl, George, *Foundations of Morality*.
1 871871 27 1   £17.95 (Autumn 1999).

Frankl, George, *Archaeology of the Mind*.
1 871871 16 6   pbk/£8.95

Frankl, George, *The Unknown Self*.
1 871871 18 2   pbk/£7.95

Wynne-Tyson, E., *Mithras*.
0 900000 79 1   £20.00

Wynne-Tyson, E., *The Philosophy of Compassion*.
0 900000 72 4   £10.00

Lancaster, C., *The Incredible World's Parliament
of Religions*.
At the Chicago Columbian Exposition of 1893.
A Comparative and Critical Study.
0 900000 25 9   £22.00

Schonfield, Hugh J., *Proclaiming the Messiah:
The Life and Letters of Paul of Tarsus,
Envoy to the Nations*.
1 871871 32 8   £9.95/ $18.95

Schonfield, Hugh J., *The Mystery of the Messiah*.
1 871871 38 7   £8.95/ $16.95

OPEN GATE PRESS

51 Achilles Road, London NW6 1DZ England
Tel: (+44) 0171 431 4391 Fax: (+44) 0171 431 5088
e-mail: books@opengatepress.co.uk